FORECASTING MAINSTREAM SCHOOL FUNDING

JULIE CORDINER

NIKOLA FLINT

SCHOOL FINANCIAL SUCCESS

ISBN-13: 978-0995590250

CONTENTS

1

INTRODUCTION

Are you a mainstream school leader and are you worrying about your budget? Do you find the school funding system complex and uncertain? How can you tell if the plans you've made to achieve your vision are affordable, without any meaningful indications of your future allocations?

Strategic financial planning is an essential part of leadership. But it seems to become more difficult every year. The school funding system keeps changing, cost pressures are building up all the time, and with every round of pay awards, the government takes different decisions on how much of an increase schools can afford to absorb.

You are expected to be in control of the school's finances, yet there are so many areas which you can't influence. The amount of funding you receive is one of these. If we boil it down to its simplest level, it comprises two main elements: the number of pupils you have, and the amount of money each one attracts.

Each of these two elements is beset by uncertainties. In relation to pupil numbers, there are many issues governing admissions to your school, and you could find that once pupils are admitted, they don't all stay until the normal transition point.

When it comes to the level of funding you receive for each pupil, your allocations partly depend on the DfE's success in competing with other government departments to secure an adequate level of funding for schools. This process is called a Spending Review, leading to the Treasury setting out government spending plans, often (but not always) over a three-year period. But there are annual fluctuations too, arising from decisions by Ministers on the implementation of school funding policy.

The National Funding Formula (NFF) has been introduced as a mechanism to distribute money between schools more fairly, to tackle the historic imbalance which has caused different levels of funding in schools with relatively similar profiles. But it will take a very long time to achieve the long-term aim, because of the need to offer protections for schools who would lose a lot of money if the pure formula was allowed to run unchecked.

The ever-present economic difficulties and the complexity of these policies mean that the government is rarely able to offer meaningful indications of school funding allocations for more than one year at a time.

Given these issues, one of the challenges of the English school funding system is that leaders are expected to plan ahead and manage very large budgets in a high-stakes accountability system with virtually no information about how much money they might receive beyond the current year.

*Your future funding is the missing piece of
the forward planning jigsaw.*

The reality

The result of the above tensions is that you're expected to do a huge amount with the limited resources you are given. Schools can't focus solely on delivering lessons; they have to play a part in ensuring pupils are ready to learn, and that often means an involvement in every aspect of children's lives. This will vary depending on the nature of the community you serve. All schools have their difficulties, but where there is a high level of disadvantage and/or special educational needs, the challenges will be even greater.

The support that used to be available via preventative and early help services has been significantly reduced or has even disappeared in many areas as a result of the austerity cuts imposed from 2010. But the problems haven't gone away; in many places, they've become significantly worse. Schools are left to pick up the pieces and do what they can to support their pupils.

New duties sometimes arise, which rarely come with additional funding; school leaders are expected to absorb them within their existing resources. Just look at the impact of Covid-19 and the limited funding provided by the government compared to the actual costs incurred by many schools.

It's incredibly difficult to make plans to achieve your vision and deliver your statutory responsibilities when you don't know how much funding will be available in the future. Lurching from one year to the next is not a reliable basis for a budget and it makes long-term planning incredibly difficult, as the data for schools in deficit demonstrates.

Schools in deficit

Some leaders feel that there is little point in even trying to build predictions of their future funding, due to all the uncertainties. They say that they simply don't have the information on which to base their forecasts, so they will just try to ride it out and wait for more concrete information. Sometimes governors won't challenge this theory, because they are understandably uncomfortable with the prospect of restructuring and potential job losses.

The trouble with this line of thinking is that it doesn't take very long to send a school budget spiralling into deficit, but it can take a prolonged period of hard work and some very painful decisions in order to climb out of it, especially if you leave it too late.

In recent years, the proportion of schools in deficit has risen, mainly due to funding not keeping pace with cost pressures (especially in the period from 2015 to 2018). The most reliable statistics at individual school level are for local authority maintained schools. The overall number of LA schools included in the data reduces over time through academy conversions, but this doesn't necessarily affect the proportion in deficit.

The reason the LA school data is more reliable is that the statistics for academy data can only be published at the level of the trust, which is the legal entity. Therefore they include only one figure for each multi-academy trust (MAT). They appear to have a lower rate of deficits in the official statistics, but this is understated, because academies in deficit are not counted if their MAT has an overall surplus. It's also not possible to identify the levels of top-slicing and pooling of General Annual Grant (GAG) by trusts, which can obscure the real situation in individual academies.

Various surveys tell us that the pressures are similar between both systems. That's only to be expected: the funding is based on the same principles, and both academies and LA maintained schools are facing similar cost increases in providing statutory education.

Returning to the evidence on LA maintained schools, the following table shows the proportion of schools with a **cumulative** deficit between 2015/16 and 2018/19 (the latest data at the time of writing). This reveals the impact of inadequate resourcing over this period. The average funding per pupil was more or less static, but pay and pension contribution increases caused significant pressures.

Figure 1: Proportion of LA schools with cumulative deficits 2015/16 to 2018/19

	2015/16	2016/17	2017/18	2018/19
Primary	5%	7%	8%	8%
Secondary	18%	26%	30%	28%
Special	8%	11%	10%	13%

If we look at **in-year** deficits, i.e. overspending against a single-year budget, the position is significantly worse. In the year ended 31st March 2019, more than 40% of schools in most phases were either eating into reserves, falling into deficit or increasing an existing deficit. The average deficit per school is also worrying.

Figure 2: Proportion of LA schools with an in-year deficit in 2018/19

	% with an in-year deficit	Average deficit per school
Primary	43.3%	£36,439
Secondary	45.0%	£166,084
All-through	34.5%	£280,243
Special	47.8%	£92,557

These statistics suggest that the financial planning methods used in the past may not have provided sufficient advance warning of the looming gap between funding and expenditure. Our experience of working with schools in financial difficulty has confirmed that aside from cost pressures, another factor that can lead to a deficit is an unrealistic assumption about future funding.

The information gap

The fundamental problem is the lack of meaningful information about the level of funding for education in future years. The initial announcement of a three-year settlement for 2020/21 to 2022/23 in the Dedicated Schools Grant (DSG) was a step forward, providing around £7.1bn extra by 2022/23 compared to 2019/20. But this increase is at a national level; the announcement did not shed any light on how the additional funding would be distributed.

One important question is how much of the extra funding will be eaten up by rising pupil numbers (especially in the secondary sector) and by pay and price increases up to March 2023.

Another concern is how the huge pressures on funding for special educational needs will be resolved. In the first two years of this latest settlement, £1.5bn of the total £4.8bn increase has been allocated to the High Needs Block. This sounds substantial (especially after the limited increases in the previous three years) and in percentage terms it's similar to the rate at which the number of Education, Health & Care Plans (EHCPs) has increased in the last couple of years.

However, the costs of providing places and support for these children and young people are also rising, so it may not be enough. In addition, there are large cumulative High Needs deficits in many LAs which need to be addressed at some point.

Any further shift towards the High Needs Block could have a significant impact on mainstream schools' core funding, which comes from the Schools Block. The DfE is putting all its eggs in a SEND Review basket, but at the time of writing, this has been delayed and is not expected to report until early 2021. This means there will not be any realignment of funding between the blocks until 2022/23 at the earliest, creating even more uncertainty.

Producing your own forecasts

In the absence of any reliable information about your future funding, the only sensible solution is to estimate it yourself, using a broad-brush approach based on a set of reasonable assumptions. It's the foundation of your multi-year budget, so it's important to give it some careful thought.

The aim of this book is to suggest an approach to help you construct your own funding forecasts. It will provide a model which you can follow if you wish, or you can create your own. Whichever method you adopt, you'll find guidance on the issues to consider when setting out the assumptions on which your forecasts are based.

What we'll cover

The book follows a logical progression, providing the context, the rationale and the steps to take to produce your funding forecasts:

- Why attempt funding forecasts? The context and challenges of medium-term budgeting.
- Scenario planning: what it is, what the benefits are, and how to apply it to your future funding.
- An overview of the approach to forecasting your funding: the main components of the model.
- Pupil number assumptions: how to gather and interpret information to underpin the model.
- Pupil number projections: choosing your best, middle and worst-case options.
- The context for per-pupil funding: making sense of the National Funding Formula.
- Per-pupil funding assumptions: how to interpret the available information.
- Per-pupil funding projections: choosing your best, middle and worst-case options.

- Combining the options: identifying nine possible permutations of pupil numbers and per-pupil funding.
- Choosing three scenarios: narrowing down from nine options to three scenarios for your core funding, which you will develop further.
- Pupil Premium: assumptions and projections.
- Other funding sources: assumptions for specific grants.
- Preparing your final scenarios: drawing everything together to produce best, middle and worst-case scenarios to transfer into your budget planning software.
- Your Financial Sustainability Plan: getting approval for revised budget plans based on your funding forecasts, and deciding how to respond to any projected shortfall or surplus.
- Conclusions: a summary of the process and results.

This book focuses on forecasting funding. You'll find lots of information on the budget planning part of the process in our other books, School Budget Mastery and Leading a School Budget Review. All the details can be found at https://schoolfinancialsuccess.com/book-table/.

Using the book

How you use this book is up to you. You can read through the narrative to understand the principles, then use our guidance and tips to develop your own forecasting model. Alternatively, you can follow our end-to-end process in a downloadable PDF with screenshots of our sample model. You'll find a link to download it in chapter 4, along with another PDF containing clickable links for all the URLs mentioned in the book.

The activities to build the model are signposted with this icon:

The end of the activity will be marked with a line of asterisks like this:

* * *

Constructing the model

It isn't possible to provide an Excel workbook with this book for technical reasons, but building the model yourself is an invaluable exercise; it enhances your understanding and will allow you to tailor it. Some of the activities may be best carried out by specific members of staff, because they will require different skills. Some are objective, mathematical and technical, though they should be within the grasp of anyone with ordinary numeracy skills. Others need a more subjective approach.

It's important to make sure that those who are involved in developing the model have sufficient time and support to work on it. The inputs will determine the results, so quality time is needed to achieve a meaningful set of forecasts.

Regardless of who completes the activities, it is important to discuss the results with the leadership team and governors. Each stage builds on the one before, so try to secure a debate about your findings as you go. You'll find it beneficial if you can arrange some planning time as a team to test the assumptions, confirm the conclusions and discuss what the results mean for your school. If new information becomes available, it will be easy to change the model, but this should be by agreement.

Your discussions will help everyone's professional development, as well as being a way of achieving a common understanding of the challenges and ownership of the solutions. It's far better to engage everyone in the development of the forecasts than face a barrage of questions at the very end of the process, or even be asked to go back to square one!

Creating a Financial Sustainability Plan

Towards the end of this book you will see a recommendation to construct a Financial Sustainability Plan (FSP). In this plan, you will outline the results of your work, recording the approach you've taken and the basis of the assumptions behind your forecasts. It will propose actions to address any shortfall between the funding forecasts and planned expenditure, or to invest in improved outcomes if you have a surplus, all in line with your educational vision for the school.

This may not be as time-consuming as you might think. As you go through the activities, you will gradually build up a portfolio of evidence, assumptions and findings, which will form the basis of your FSP. The final stage will involve presenting it all and working with your colleagues to identify solutions for the issues that emerge.

The FSP is a helpful tool for achieving engagement across your team and governing board or trust, to help you tackle the financial challenges you are facing. It can also be used to provide evidence to your funding body and other stakeholders, helping them to see that you have a robust strategy to deal with any future financial challenges.

Keeping the model current

You can roll forward the model to achieve an ongoing set of forecasts as each new financial year approaches. To facilitate this, the instructions for the model are couched in general terms, starting with the baseline year and forecasting years 1, 2 and 3.

This book contains advice on how to build the model in both stages of the National Funding Formula (Soft and Hard NFF, as we'll explain short-ly), given the current uncertainty over timescales for the full reforms to be implemented. It shows you how to find information and assess the impact of any changes, helping you choose the best approach at that time.

While we've done our best to present the contents in a way that will help you to roll the model forward, we hope you will understand how difficult it is to cover every eventuality! You will therefore need to check whether there are any changes in the way the NFF operates in future years. They may affect your assumptions or require slight changes in the way the model works.

The best way to stay informed about future changes to the school funding system is to sign up to the School Financial Success newsletter via the home page at https://schoolfinancialsuccess.com, and follow the monthly blog, where you'll find information on any new developments.

2

WHY ATTEMPT FUNDING FORECASTS?

Strong financial leadership

Taking a strategic view of your school's finances is more important than ever in these challenging times. A light-touch approach may have been sufficient in the dim and distant past, when budgets were relatively stable. With so much uncertainty around the current school funding arrangements, there is a need for higher-level financial leadership skills to deal with the wide-ranging changes that lie ahead.

Strategic financial planning is an important aspect of financial leadership. It means taking a longer-term view in order to achieve some stability, managing your resources beyond a single year to achieve financial sustainability.

The government has recognised this and now requires all schools to submit a three-year budget plan, following a consultation on improving financial transparency. There's a certain irony in this when the DfE can't provide multi-year allocations, but it is a necessary element in forward planning, so you have to do it as best you can.

You will have a clear vision for what you want to achieve over the medium term, and your financial decisions are a vital part of making those plans happen. Ensuring the school's resources are targeted to your priorities is always important, but especially so when funding isn't keeping pace with your need to spend.

This means that your medium-term financial plan should be linked to your school improvement plan. But if you haven't put much thought into how much money you are likely to receive in future, any attempt at a three-year plan is likely to be little more than aspirational guesswork.

Your three-year funding forecasts are therefore the foundation of this financial plan. How else will you know if your plans are going to be affordable?

Early warning system

As you've already seen in the introductory chapter, you cannot rely on the government to provide meaningful indications of your future funding. Your best approach is to take control yourself and devise an early warning system to reduce the risk of a deficit, or help you in turning round an existing deficit.

Making an attempt at forecasting your funding will help you to understand how sensitive it is to external factors. You'll see the difference that developments such as changes in pupil numbers and the progression of the National Funding Formula (NFF) could make to your future allocations.

Constructing a medium-term financial plan with robust funding forecasts will mean you can react quickly to any unexpected events. You might be able to achieve earlier savings through staff turnover or opportunities for lower prices when re-tendering contracts. You will know what to do when these happen, because you have worked out where you need to be by a certain date.

Alternatively, something might happen that causes an overspend, for example the need to offer recruitment and retention allowances, spikes in staff sickness or maternity, or emergency building repairs. Building your forecasts and FSP will prompt you to find solutions to a worst-case scenario of a major shortfall in funding, so you can generate ideas in advance on how you might respond to these sorts of events. The aim is to create some flexibility in your spending plans, so you can pivot quickly to solve problems as soon as they occur. The need for this has been particularly evident during the Covid-19 pandemic.

Fundamentally, having a plan based on a set of assumptions means that you won't have to start from scratch with your decision-making every time something changes. Whatever the reasons behind the new developments, it will simply be a matter of tweaking the assumptions in your plan to reflect the new information. Once created, the model will only require minimal input; any changes to pupil numbers or per-pupil funding should automatically flow through to the final scenarios.

Assurance

Schools are funded from the public purse, so you're accountable for how the grants received are spent. Funding bodies (local authorities and the Education and Skills Funding Agency) are required to monitor schools in order to obtain assurance that they are financially sustainable.

The framework for the monitoring of school finances is set out in key documents which outline the relationship between schools and their funding bodies. They detail the required financial arrangements and the information that schools have to provide through the submission of returns and reports. For LA maintained schools, the key documents are the local Scheme for Financing Schools and council Financial Regulations. Academies must observe the Academies Financial Handbook and their own funding agreements.

Funding body actions

If a school or academy can't balance the budget, it is required to notify its funding body, who will swing into action to reduce the risk by applying their formal procedures.

What does this mean? Let's look at academies first. A multi-academy trust (MAT) is expected to manage academy deficits within the trust's overall financial envelope. Unless there is a really solid culture of mutual support, trustees could face disgruntled leaders from other academies who are asked to give up reserves or pay an increased top slice to underwrite another academy's deficit while a recovery plan is implemented.

Some MATs operate pooling of General Annual Grant (GAG). This means that the trust can aggregate some or all of the GAG for its academies and redistribute it according to need. The only element which can't be pooled is Private Finance Initiative funding. A minority of trusts practise pooling, but surveys often suggest more are considering it. If it's a policy in your trust, we recommend that you talk to your central team, as it may not be worth your while to attempt forecasts if your formula allocation won't be passed on intact, even under direct funding from the DfE.

If a MAT or single academy trust goes into deficit, or there are serious concerns about other aspects of its financial management, the ESFA will issue a financial notice to improve. This usually results in the automatic withdrawal of delegation, involving the removal of financial decision-making powers from the trust or academy until matters are resolved to the ESFA's satisfaction, which may involve a recovery plan.

The response to deficits is similar for local authority maintained schools. LAs will expect their schools to produce a recovery plan, usually to bring the budget into balance within three years. They can also issue warning notices and withdraw delegation if they don't have confidence in the school's recovery plan. We cover this in more detail in 'School Budget Mastery', the first in the School Financial Success Guides series.

Staying in control

Whichever route you end up following, being in deficit is not a pleasant experience. It must surely be better for you, your staff and pupils to stay in control of your school's destiny and get things working in line with your original vision. This will still involve difficult decisions, but you will decide the approach and determine the pace of change.

If you are being proactive by developing financial forecasts based on a robust set of assumptions, your funding body should be reassured, and if you take action to avoid future problems, you'll be less likely to end up on a 'watch list'.

There is also a tactical reason to improve, in terms of supporting the schools sector as a whole. As long as the DfE can identify cases of financial mismanagement, waste, and a failure of some schools to take action early enough to prevent deficits, it will be much more difficult to argue that current levels of funding are insufficient. The Secretary of State will therefore struggle to make the case to the Treasury for more money in a future Spending Review, which determines the level of resources available to education. Excessively high balances (far greater than a normal working reserve) can also cause the same problem; forward planning will help you to ensure that funding is used for the pupils currently in school.

Be realistic about the challenges and try to manage everyone's expectations. We'll say more about this in chapter 3, but the essence is getting colleagues and governors to realise that given all the possibilities and uncertainties, it can only be a high-level forecast, based on a reasonable set of assumptions. A sensible method like this has to be better than pure guesswork.

If you get this right, you'll be regarded as a proactive, responsible leader who's taking action to achieve a sustainable budget which supports improved outcomes.

Key points

- Funding forecasts demonstrate strong financial leadership, making a required three-year budget plan meaningful and ensuring your plans will be affordable.
- They provide an early warning system to indicate the sensitivity of your funding to changes that are outside of your control. You can be ready to take advantage of changes and achieve early savings where possible, having thought about your response to different levels of funding.
- Forecasts allow you to provide assurance of the school's financial sustainability to your funding body and supply evidence of robust assumptions supported by SLT and governors.
- By being proactive, you can avoid the loss of control that comes with falling into deficit, where your funding body may put close monitoring in place or even withdraw delegation.

3

SCENARIO PLANNING

What is scenario planning?

We've already established that in the absence of any meaningful information about your future funding, it's best to develop your own method for making forecasts. This might sound ambitious, but as long as you devise a set of robust assumptions, it is possible to put together some reasonable estimates that you can justify.

There will inevitably be a margin of error in any forecasting, so we advocate scenario planning, which recognises that the future is uncertain.

Scenario planning is a helpful and flexible technique where you present options for the future, in order to stimulate a constructive debate about how your organisation might respond to different circumstances.

Anticipating future developments and communicating them clearly can be challenging, but this approach helps leaders to explain the impact of a range of possibilities. It will also mean you are better prepared should any of them materialise. This sort of approach recognises that the future is uncertain, and that your plans can be affected by external influences that you have absolutely no control over.

Scenarios need to be built on a set of assumptions, which should be discussed with those who are involved in decision-making. They can make a fundamental difference to the results, so careful thought is needed when developing and agreeing them.

Most people using this technique develop three scenarios: best case, middle case and worst-case:

- **Best-case scenario:** an optimistic one. It may not happen, but it allows you to be ambitious and forward-thinking. How could you use any additional funding to secure better outcomes or to better manage cost pressures? Or if the NFF is detrimental to your finances, what is the least damaging option?
- **Middle-case scenario:** the most realistic one. It will reflect your local knowledge of your local authority's potential decisions on the formula while they still have discretion, the DfE's approach to school funding policy, and how your pupil numbers might change over the next three years.
- **Worst-case scenario:** your doomsday version, the least possible funding over the next three years. You hope that this scenario won't happen, but you need to allow for the possibility and be ready with plans to help you cope if it does.

There should be a reasonable gap between each of the three scenarios, to make it worth your while to draw up plans for coping with them.

Using scenario planning for school funding forecasts

So, how can scenario planning be used to forecast your school's funding? This technique can help you see how sensitive your funding is to changes in government policy or funding systems. It can be used to test out different combinations of the two main components of your funding: pupil numbers and the amount of money you receive for each pupil.

Pupil numbers are an important determinant of your funding because that's how most of the money in the NFF is shared out. In 2020/21, the average proportion of the total money which was allocated on pupil-led factors (rolls and pupil characteristics) across all LA formulae was 90.4%. This is expected to increase when the teachers' pay and pension grants are added into the Schools NFF from 2021/22. Most other grants also rely on pupil numbers and characteristics to varying extents.

Your intake and the number of leavers will therefore continue to be important, as will pupil mobility if it is a feature of your school.

The amount of money you receive for each pupil is affected by the total funding allocated by the government and by the school funding reforms which have created the National Funding Formula. The NFF appears complex, but there are some features and advance information which can be used to identify the worst-case option for your future funding as a starting point. You will find a full explanation of this in chapter 7.

Scenario planning is a flexible method which you can use to produce high-level forecasts of your future funding. It supports medium-term financial planning by helping you to identify three different funding levels across the next three years which you can place into your budget planning system as alternative scenarios.

By comparing these funding scenarios with your proposed levels of expenditure across the same period, it will highlight whether you are likely to face a shortfall or not. You'll be able to identify either the level of savings needed to achieve a balanced budget over the next three years, or (if you're lucky) the extra funding that will be available to meet cost pressures, improve outcomes and/or deal with the impact of rising rolls, whichever is relevant to your situation. Either way, this approach will help you to decide on the most efficient and effective deployment of the available funding and will guide your plan to achieve a balanced budget.

Once you have an idea of whether you could be facing a shortfall or not, you can start thinking about how you would respond, creating a robust set of proposals for your three-year budget plan. This is much better than pure guesswork or adding inflation to your existing funding, either of which could give a false impression of your future financial position and send you into deficit.

Scenario planning in MATs

If you are an academy in a MAT with a high level of autonomy over finance, you can prepare your own forecasts. If you are working for the trust, we advise you to develop scenarios for each individual academy. While it's easy to aggregate pupil numbers to trust level, each academy can attract very different levels of per-pupil funding. You can then aggregate the results and consider your top-slicing or GAG pooling approach. This will aid your medium-term planning for the trust as a whole.

This process may spark new ideas about how the trust's overall funding might change. It could also influence your priorities for investment in relation to supporting specific academies or trust-wide improvement, based on your assumptions about issues such as performance, workforce strategy, centralisation of services and procurement policies.

Before going further into the application of scenario planning, let's look more closely at the benefits of this technique.

What are the benefits?

There are many benefits to scenario planning as a means of forecasting your funding. The main people who form your audience when you're preparing funding forecasts are your colleagues in the senior leadership team, governors and your funding body. Each will be involved to a different degree, but it can be helpful to think about the process from their point of view as well as your own.

1. Demonstrating financial sustainability

One pragmatic benefit of scenario planning is that it fulfils the expectations of your funding body that you will manage your delegated funding responsibly and prepare robust multi-year budget projections to prove that the school is financially secure. We've already mentioned the requirement to submit a three-year budget plan; this technique makes it meaningful, rather than a tick-in-the-box exercise.

Your funding body needs to know that you are not going to plunge into deficit, and that you have a strategic plan to manage any changes in funding or spending requirements. To achieve this reassurance, they have written various conditions into the documents that govern your relationship with them, which we've already mentioned: the LA Scheme and Financial Regulations, or the Academy Financial Handbook and individual funding agreements. Demonstrating that you've gone through a proper process helps to build your funding body's confidence in your ability to create and maintain a strategic plan. Scenario planning provides that proper process.

Aside from the legal requirement, knowing the school is financially secure is important for you as a leader, as part of your delegated responsibility for finance. Planning for only one year at a time is not a helpful practice; it engenders a feeling of being out of control. As you work through the process of building scenarios, you can record your assumptions and decisions along with the outcomes, ready for when you need to draw it all together and present it in a Financial Sustainability Plan.

The process can also build confidence among staff, governors and other key stakeholders. They will see that you have a plan in place to handle any future changes which might have an adverse impact on the school. At a time when staff retention is so important, you need to avoid any nervousness about whether jobs might be at risk if leaders fail to plan ahead properly.

2. Reducing the burden of expectation

Expectations on school leaders are high. Staff will be looking to you for guidance and reassurance about their future employment and the direction in which the school is going. They may think that you have all the answers, and the weight of that expectation can be heavy.

You probably feel as if there is a pressure on you to produce accurate predictions in every aspect of your budget, but you know it's not that simple, especially in relation to your future funding. If you have already tried to produce a three-year budget forecast, you'll know what it feels like.

Scenario planning reduces this burden by helping interested parties to realise that it isn't that straightforward to predict your funding. The information you'll produce will demonstrate that there are lots of external influences which might send your figures in either direction. Well-managed debates about the assumptions will reinforce this.

The whole exercise is done at a high level; taking a broad-brush approach to the underpinning assumptions should reduce the expectation of accuracy. This can bring a sense of freedom and relief.

3. Handling uncertainty

Scenario planning encourages you to deal with the uncertainties around your future funding by pulling apart the different components and examining how they could change. Understanding the impact of different options for rolls, pupil characteristics and the level of funding per pupil provides an insight into the sensitivity of your funding.

This approach will expose areas where you are more reliant on particular funding streams, such as those which are targeted towards deprivation or low prior attainment. If your local authority (LA) is moving its school funding formula towards the NFF, changes in the values for these factors could affect you. Alternatively, you might realise that difficulties in securing an adequate level of funding for pupils with SEND from the local authority's High Needs Budget are playing a vital part in your struggles.

If you are a relatively small school, the exercise will expose the importance of the lump sum and the challenges that variations in pupil numbers can bring. There are many other features which can make funding uncertain in different types of school; scenario planning often brings these to the fore and it can be helpful to discuss them.

Many changes will be outside of your control, so they are difficult to predict. But it's important to identify those that you can influence, such as reviewing your curriculum offer, or improving parental perceptions by working with the LA's media team or local press and radio stations to find ways of getting good news stories into local media in a targeted way.

Putting effort into identifying your scenarios and stating the assumptions that underpin them is a strategic exercise, but it has a real purpose in a pragmatic sense. It helps you to consider the impact of different levels of funding and decide how you would respond to each of them. Your plans become a working document which is referred to and updated on a regular basis as more information becomes available.

This is all much more meaningful than a 'finger in the wind' exercise. You are choosing to examine your future financial position proactively and professionally, rather than producing a rough three-year plan because someone else has told you to do it.

A plan that is done grudgingly is likely to be submitted then shelved for another year because it isn't owned. Your plan, on the other hand, will be the outcome of deep thought and collaborative work with your key stakeholders, creating a blueprint for your future financial success.

4. Opening up debate

One of the most valuable benefits of scenario planning is that you can create the opportunity to stimulate a real debate about how the school would respond if the amount of money coming in from government changed significantly, either for better or for worse.

To achieve realistic scenarios, you need to form robust assumptions about the different elements of your funding. It helps to be honest about whether you are being overly optimistic or pessimistic, and whether you even have a realistic option on the table as a result of your choices. You'll need to test them out with colleagues and governors to make sure they are workable.

This will produce some interesting debates, such as people's beliefs about why parents decide to apply for a place at your school or not. It could also bring out some useful information that you might not be aware of, such as another school's plans for expansion that governors know about through their links with the community.

When the whole of your Senior Leadership Team (SLT) and all governors can see the options for the school's future funding and have to consider how they would respond to them, it should open up a debate that focuses attention on the things that matter. It is human nature to keep doing things because we've always done them, because we like to stay within our comfort zone. But true learning happens outside your comfort zone.

If things which are regarded as important are placed under threat, people start to think creatively about how to preserve them. The debate can expose differences in opinion, and some leaders or governors may challenge whether a particular practice is still relevant or effective. This is healthy, because it gets to the heart of value for money considerations.

The process can encourage a collaborative approach. Starting early with a high-level analysis creates time and space to stimulate creative thinking. Take the opportunity to involve the whole school in considering different ways of working to achieve the changes that are necessary. This could include time-saving ideas, cost reductions, fund-raising ventures or relationships with local businesses or community organisations that bring benefits, either monetary or in-kind. You're not the only one who can have bright ideas!

You are bound to get a wide range of views when you start talking about potential outcomes and solutions to make your future budgets work, whether that's at a very high level for a wider audience, or at a detailed level with individual budget holders.

This is where cultural issues can come to the fore. What is your attitude to money? Is it different from the attitude of the rest of your leadership team, or the governors on the Governing Board and Finance Committee? Are some of your staff or governors averse to planning, preferring to take a more laissez-faire approach? Getting a consensus can be tricky if there are a lot of subjective views on the topic. But at least scenario planning gives you a vehicle to explore them in a transparent way before coming to a decision.

5. Easier decision-making

Once you have developed your three-year budget plan and identified actions to take to achieve financial sustainability, your plan will provide a basis for any future decisions. This is not a plan to be put on the shelf and forgotten about. It's not set in stone; you can and should update it as more information emerges.

Reviewing your forecasts periodically is important. If you follow a plan based on outdated assumptions, there's a risk of implementing savings that could later prove to be unnecessary, or of not reacting quickly enough to adverse changes when new information emerges. Keep an eye open for anything that affects the two main elements: pupil numbers and per-pupil funding. Remember that you are using broad-brush assumptions, and don't get drawn in too deeply.

The beauty of having three potential budget plans is that you can pivot quickly if circumstances change. As opportunities present themselves, such as unexpected staff turnover, you may be able to secure early savings, which could make your financial position more secure and perhaps even prevent compulsory redundancies at a later stage. That will save you a lot of time, not to mention relief when you can avoid the emotional impact of causing someone to lose their job or seeing your staff go through a difficult process.

On the other hand, if things get worse, such as the withdrawal of a grant (as happened with the Y7 Catch Up Grant) or high price increases in any of your contracts, you can consult your worst-case scenario and bring plans for finding additional savings into play.

Whichever situation you're in, there is both a time-saving and a psychological benefit: you won't have to go through a fundamental decision-making process each time your circumstances change. You have a plan to follow and can adopt or adjust the course of action you've already set. It's simply a matter of consulting your plan, taking the action and updating the document to reflect the impact.

6. Supporting continuous improvement

Scenario planning prompts you to re-examine your vision and priorities, as you identify different possibilities for your future funding. This is an invaluable process that will support your ongoing school development plan (SDP) and help you to achieve continuous improvement.

You will already be aware of the need to re-evaluate your SDP on a regular basis, given the volatile nature of events in the education sector in recent times. But when you're linking your improvement plan with your medium-term budget, it's doubly important. Doing the same as you've always done could result in worse outcomes, financially as well as in terms of pupil progress and achievement.

As you develop your SDP and your budget plans, you'll need to consider whether your curriculum and staffing plans are still relevant. Have your data and the level of funding available been at the heart of your discussions?

It is easy to get caught up in exciting initiatives which you hope will transform outcomes for your pupils. But they need to be rooted in reality, otherwise you could end up spending money you haven't got, possibly on actions that don't actually secure improvement. You might appear to be efficient, but you could be doing the wrong things incredibly well. That won't help you achieve your vision.

Managing expectations

If you want to avoid any misunderstandings and, above all else, manage expectations, it is advisable to explain the principles of scenario planning before you start to engage staff, governors and any other stakeholders in it.

The first and most essential message is that the exercise is not guaranteed to provide an accurate prediction of your future funding. It is a broad brush set of multiple possibilities to use as a starting point for debating how the school would respond if faced with different levels of funding.

Everyone needs to understand that it is not possible to know what will happen beyond the latest settlement. The Spending Review information is at a high level and the details of how it will be shared out in line with priorities usually comes later. Until direct funding by the DfE is introduced (the so-called 'Hard NFF'), there will also be local variations in the way the funding that's passed to LAs is distributed between schools.

It's advisable to try to explain this in simple terms to your colleagues and governors when working through the assumptions for your model. They need to accept that there will be a margin of error. But you will be able to firm up figures as more information emerges.

Scenario planning involves producing a range of high-level estimates based on a set of assumptions which may or may not materialise. So another message to convey is that it is not a detailed calculation of every element of your funding.

As we will see, there are various ways of arriving at these three estimates. Choosing your final three will be a matter of judgement. This is no different to your usual practice in questioning and deciding the expenditure and self-generated income elements of your three-year forward plan.

Everyone involved in discussing the scenarios needs to take responsibility for understanding and challenging the assumptions you have made. If any of these are patently unrealistic, i.e. wildly optimistic or pessimistic, or if they rely on an unlikely combination of events, it would be unwise to base decisions on them.

There is a huge temptation to make the results fit what you would like the scenarios to be. We urge you to resist this idea. Let the results speak for themselves, once you have made an honest assessment of the likely change in your per-pupil funding and rolls. It may be an eye-opener.

Your assumptions may also need to change as decisions are taken by other parties, notably the DfE and your local authority. Even when LAs are no longer responsible for distributing school funding via a local formula, there will be areas of funding which they will still control, particularly early years and high needs, unless there is a major change in the funding arrangements. Revisiting the assumptions at regular intervals will help to ensure that your plans are still on track.

Key points

- Scenario planning is a flexible technique which presents options for the future to stimulate a constructive debate about how to respond.
- It usually involves three scenarios: best, middle and worst-case.
- You can apply it by using pupil numbers and funding per-pupil for school funding forecasts.
- The main benefits are demonstrating financial sustainability, reducing the burden of expectation, handling uncertainty, opening up debate, easier decision-making and supporting continuous improvement.
- It's important to manage expectations, so everyone understands it can't be an accurate prediction but rather a broad brush set of possibilities, and that the underpinning assumptions are very important.

4
___

AN OVERVIEW OF THE FORECASTING MODEL

The key elements

This is not just a book; it's a practical toolkit which you can follow in order to produce three scenarios for your future funding as the basis of your three-year budget plan. In this chapter, we will explain the basic elements of the model, the information you need to make a start, and the ways in which you can tailor the model to suit your own preferences. We will also share some tips on how to build it.

On the face of it, the task of forecasting funding is relatively straightforward if we reduce it to the key elements of the school funding system. As we said earlier, these are the number of pupils you have and the average amount you receive for each one.

There are lots of complications in the school funding system if you delve into it. However, the purpose of your forecast is to raise awareness of the scope for changes in your funding, to stimulate debate and provide a basis for your strategic planning. So, let's keep it as simple as possible.

The reason for this level of simplicity will become clear as we start to develop the model. It quite quickly becomes multi-dimensional, because you will not only be considering three different options for rolls and per-pupil funding, but you will also need to project your forecasts over a period of three years.

To explain the model, we have adopted a terminology of options and scenarios. Options are produced in the early stages, when you identify your best, middle and worst-case estimates of per-pupil funding and rolls as separate exercises. Scenarios are produced when you combine the options by multiplying them together.

You will build the model in stages, firstly focusing on the most significant area: budget share (the first line of the academy GAG statement). Once you have established three scenarios for this element, you will add in other sources of funding.

Although the initial steps may seem detailed, they set helpful foundations. Once you've constructed the model, you will be able to roll it forward easily to achieve a continuous three-year forecast. For the majority of your funding, all you will need to do is change the baseline to reflect the most recent year's actual funding and review the percentage changes for subsequent years.

We suggest you start preparing your forecasts around three to four months before your multi-year budget plan has to be submitted. As you will see, it's wise to take time to test out your assumptions, understand the results and secure agreement from SLT colleagues and governors.

Seven steps

There are seven steps to creating a set of best, middle and worst-case scenarios for your total funding. We will guide you through these steps, but here is a summary:

1. Set your baseline rolls using the data on your funding statement for pupils in Reception to Y11, which are the pupil numbers in the October census prior to the start of the current financial year, not your current rolls.
2. Estimate the pupil numbers that will drive your funding in the following three years for best, middle and worst-case options, e.g. October 2020 for 2021/22.
3. Set your baseline funding per pupil from your latest funding

statement, focusing on the factors that relate to pupil numbers and characteristics (pupil-led funding). The rest (mainly lump sums and premises costs) will be added back later.

4. Estimate the percentage change in this pupil-led funding for the following three years for best, middle and worst-case options.
5. Multiply each of the roll options by the three £ per pupil options. This will create nine different combinations (see the diagram below) across the three years.
6. Add back the items on your funding statement that you excluded from step 3, giving a 3-year budget share projection.
7. From these nine, choose three of them and add in other funding streams to form your final scenarios for total funding. You will now be ready to transfer the results into your budget planning software, ready to work on your multi-year budget plans.

Here is a matrix depicting the potential combinations:

Figure 3: Combinations matrix

		Rolls		
		Best	Middle	Worst
£	Best	1	2	3
per	Middle	4	5	6
pupil	Worst	7	8	9

Please **do not include any self-generated income** in your per-pupil funding options, such as donations and charges for lettings and traded services. They will be deducted from your gross spending to form net expenditure, which you will compare against the funding forecasts in your budget plans. Don't double count income!

Assumptions are key

Like any other system, scenario planning is only as good as the information that you put into it. Your results will hinge on the assumptions you make about how your rolls and per-pupil funding might change.

While this could be described as a limitation, there is great value in considering and agreeing the assumptions that you are building into the model. As we discussed earlier, simply opening up the discussion about them can identify in-built attitudes and values. A well-managed healthy debate will highlight the issues to everyone involved and provide a solid platform for agreement on the actions that are needed to set your budget in the right direction.

Here are some suggestions to bear in mind:

- be clear about the assumptions that you need to make
- test them out with relevant colleagues
- consider what the margins of error might be and how they would impact on your forecasts and resulting actions
- keep the assumptions under review throughout the process.

Using the forecasts

The results of your forecasts will need to be placed into your budget planning software so you can compare them with your projected expenditure over the same period, allowing for future pay awards and other price increases. This first stage will show whether a standstill position is possible within the funding you are expecting under each scenario. This will expose any shortfalls or identify a surplus which could be used for new initiatives to secure improvement.

In the current climate, many schools will need to find savings to bring the budget into balance over the next three years. Depending on the solutions you come up with, your actions may impact upon individuals. Will your staff and governors be affected by any changes that might need to be introduced? It's better for them to be involved in the process from an early stage, then they won't need time to catch up later on.

Considering culture

The attitude towards money in your school can strongly influence your ability to set and achieve a sustainable budget. You can probably think of evidence to support this statement from your own experience; it can sometimes be difficult to persuade someone that a course of action is needed if it runs counter to their own instincts and beliefs.

In our second school funding guide, 'Leading a School Budget Review', we discuss the importance of culture and how to build engagement with all staff, governors and other stakeholders to support your endeavours in balancing the budget.

It's worth remembering that as the person initiating the forecasts, you are some way ahead of everyone else in your thinking. Others need time to absorb the information and make sense of it before they can understand what you are trying to achieve, form a view on it and be willing to play a part. So think carefully about how and when to communicate your progress and involve others.

Sharing this process with staff and governors will help them to appreciate the different ways in which your financial position might develop in a relatively short period of time. This can be a bit of a revelation to some people, who shy away from thinking too far ahead when managing their own money, and who sometimes get into difficulties as a result.

With a range of different funding options underpinning your three-year financial plan, you have an opportunity to engage more people in the debate about how to respond to any future shortfall. Allowing a reasonable amount of time for this exercise will build confidence and stimulate creative thinking, which is much better than a rushed set of decisions.

By creating a culture of openness and transparency, and valuing everyone's opinions, you can encourage people to offer their thoughts and jointly develop practical solutions. Often those who are carrying out tasks on a daily basis have a far better understanding of the potential for doing things differently and more efficiently.

Constructing the model

Before diving into the detail, it's a good idea to think about the process of constructing your forecasting model. Many of you will be comfortable using the tips in the forthcoming chapters to design your own version of it. But if you need more detail, we have prepared a downloadable PDF with a sample model showing our formulae and completed examples. It is based on a fictitious primary school but the principles can be applied to any mainstream school.

You can find it by visiting this link: https://schoolfinancialsuccess. com/wp-content/uploads/2020/12/FMSF_Model.pdf.

You can download a clickable version of this link and all the other URLs mentioned from https://schoolfinancialsuccess.com/wp-content/ uploads/2020/12/FMSF_links.pdf.

The model PDF is for your personal use in your own school, and we would ask you to respect our work by not sharing it with others who haven't bought the book. You are not permitted to distribute or exploit it for commercial purposes, such as selling the model to others.

While the PDF shows how we approached the model, it's important to tailor it to suit your own preferences and circumstances. Take time to consider what would best suit your ways of working.

We have designed the model in a way that minimises the amount of input you need to do, once you have set up the formulae. Most of the calculations feed off baseline information that you enter once, using your estimated percentage changes to build the scenarios. It's a flexible approach, which allows you to change your assumptions and see the results updating automatically.

There are many different ways of tailoring the model, either in substance or in presentation. Your school may have a house style for working documents, or you might have a personal preference for how you build spreadsheets. Some funding streams may not be particularly significant for you and won't need a detailed approach.

Please check carefully at each stage to make sure that all the calculations work and that any cross-referencing between sheets within the workbook is accurate. We can't take responsibility for any errors.

Top tips for constructing the model

- Keep notes as you go, recording any changes you make to the method. For example, if you decide not to use the formulae in the rolls projection, and wish to enter year group sizes directly, keep a note of how you have estimated them. At the appropriate time, you can then easily transfer the detailed assumptions into your Financial Sustainability Plan.

- Imagine someone else will inherit the model in the future; will they be able to follow what you've done? It may take you a while to reach the stage of producing your Financial Sustainability Plan, so it's sensible to make notes as you go. You can always leave your copy of this book for your successor, but it's advisable to draw up a local set of instructions, especially if you have tailored the model.
- Carry out a sense check of the final results. Do they look reasonable? Can you easily pinpoint the main reasons for the differences between scenarios, or do some aspects look odd? Watch out for errors in entering data or percentage changes.
- Always double check any links between cells on a sheet or between sheets in the workbook.
- Use absolute values to fix a cell in a formula where you want to copy it into other cells without losing the reference to a particular cell's value. In case you don't know this trick, pressing the F4 key once fixes both the column and row numbers, a second time fixes the row number only and a third press fixes the column number only.
- Colour code your cells where you need to enter data, so they stand out. We used different colours for input cells, referenced or calculated cells, and totals.
- If you really want to avoid messing up the file accidentally, lock cells that hold calculations and when you have finished building the model, protect the sheets with a password so that you are unable to overwrite them. You will then only be able to enter data into unlocked cells. Just don't lose the password!
- Please make sure you save your work regularly, preferably backing it up to the cloud and saving it on an external drive just to be sure.

Remember that the model isn't a fixed tool that you do once and then forget about. Being flexible is essential for financial sustainability. Whenever new information becomes available, particularly during the LA's budget setting process, you should revisit the model and consider whether the percentage changes for each year need to be amended, or whether you have selected the most appropriate three final scenarios from the nine options.

In the next chapter, we will explore the question of how to establish assumptions for your pupil number forecasting.

Key points

- The main elements are your pupil numbers and the amount per pupil you receive. You will produce three options for each of these, and when you combine them, you will form scenarios.
- There are seven steps to create your final scenarios, including core budget share funding, Pupil Premium and all other grants.
- Do not include self-generated income in your funding forecasts; this will be part of your net expenditure to compare against the funding scenarios.
- Your results will only be as good as your assumptions. Take time to discuss them and keep them under review.
- Use the forecasts to engage colleagues and give them time to understand them. It will build confidence and stimulate creative thinking, helping you find solutions to any potential shortfall.
- Think about how you wish to construct the model before diving in. Keep a note of decisions and why you have taken them, for future reference, and conduct a sense check of the results to ensure accuracy.
- You will be able to amend your assumptions at any time, to keep the model up to date.

5

PUPIL NUMBER ASSUMPTIONS

Influences on your future rolls

A full school with stable pupil numbers is the ideal situation for any school. It certainly makes forward planning easier. However, many schools have to manage a more volatile situation. Whether rolls are rising or falling, changes can cause havoc for your attempts to forecast funding. But by making some reasonable assumptions across three possible scenarios, you can consider the likely impact on your funding in the future.

Let's start with a backwards look at your previous pattern of admissions in recent years. It isn't always an indicator of future admissions, but it may identify some key influences for your consideration.

Activity 1: Identifying previous pupil number trends

Try to spend a little time analysing previous trends in pupil numbers, looking backwards to see if you can identify a pattern related to particular events or local circumstances. As we'll soon see, influences may be external or internal. Ask yourself questions like these:

- How have your admission trends changed in recent years?
- Do you understand why any changes have happened?
- Can your trends in applications for places over the last five years be considered a reliable predictor of future admissions?

Make a note of your answers; they may act as useful prompts as you work through the process of projecting your future rolls.

* * *

Now it's time to consider the potential reasons for changes in pupil numbers, to inform your forecasts over the next three years. Your answers to the questions above may have identified some of them already.

To create reasonable assumptions, you will want to use a variety of sources of information. Some will come from national and local government sources. But your own local knowledge is also valuable.

There are many reasons why a school's roll can go up or down, and not all of them can be predicted. There are four main areas:

- Demographic trends
- Competition for pupils
- Pupil movement, including changes in housing provision
- Parental perceptions

Let's look at each of these in turn and consider how you can incorporate them into your estimates of future pupil numbers.

Demographic trends

The number of pupils and their characteristics play a vital part in your funding, as we've already discussed. It's therefore worth giving consideration to the issue of demographic trends.

We don't advise going into too much detail; all you're doing is trying to establish some high-level influences on your future rolls. For example, there could be a notable downturn in the local birth rate over the last two to three years, which could have an impact on the number of children in the area who will need places when they reach statutory school age. Knowing this will act as an alert, allowing you to be suitably cautious in your forecasts.

Consider the characteristics of your pupils too, particularly in relation to disadvantage. The local economy is an important influence. Changes in the mix of businesses in your area can either bring jobs or cause rising unemployment, which in turn may affect the number in poverty. The deprivation element within your core funding is more a matter for the per-pupil funding chapter, but you will want to consider free school meal eligibility rates as part of your forecasting for funding streams such as Pupil Premium and possibly some other grants.

Local authority intelligence

Education is such a fast-changing world that you can't possibly be expected to know everything. Making connections with people who know a lot about a small aspect is vital; your role is to piece together the available information and start to make some sense of it all in your particular context. Place planning is a good example of this.

Local authorities have a statutory duty to ensure there are sufficient school places, so they have a lot of information at their fingertips. They understand all the statistical information about birth rates, housing yields (such as the rate of family occupancy), and cross-boundary movement between schools, and they should be happy to share information. Their pupil projections work involves taking a lot of different perspectives into account, from analysing national data on population projections published by the Office for National Statistics to considering the local context.

It can be trickier to achieve accuracy the lower down the levels you go, because as we'll soon see, there are so many influences on admissions to individual schools. Some LAs are better at forecasting demographic trends than others, so it's advisable to ask how accurate their predictions have been in recent years.

Councils with education responsibilities usually provide pupil number predictions at a locality level to help schools with their forward planning. Your local School Place Planning officer or School Organisation lead is a valuable contact, due to their expertise and knowledge not only in relation to area-wide trends, but also the pattern of demand for places in clusters or at individual school level.

The LA is responsible for place planning across all types of school. Academies therefore have as much right as LA schools to ask for information. But how you use the intelligence is your responsibility.

Similarly, your LA's Admissions team will have a sense of trends in parental preference. The LA should be keeping headteachers informed about applications and the proportion of preferences that were met. This will help you identify the most popular schools and any changing trends in pupil numbers, including in-year transfers between schools.

If this flow of information isn't happening, talk to your Schools Forum representative or a headteacher who is on one of the LA groups that give access to senior officers, and ask them to raise it.

School-based intelligence

Staff throughout the school should have some knowledge of the families your existing pupils come from, so make use of it. Find out if your existing pupils have siblings who may want a place. This can provide a core set of pupil numbers that are reasonably reliable.

We'll look at parental preference shortly, but if you have a reliable pattern of applications from other education settings in the area, whether you consider them feeder/partner schools or not, you can use this information in your assumptions. It's always worth building a relationship with them, because impressions can be given by a pupil's current school and having them onside is helpful.

Competition

Do you face competition from other schools in your local area? It can be a difficult issue, especially if some schools engage in proactive marketing. Here are a few areas where you might see differences between schools which could influence applications for places:

- Ethos - appealing to a particular section of the community, such as faith schools, or promoting a particular set of values.
- Outcomes - you can be sure that if a nearby school has a particularly impressive set of exam results, they will publicise them and draw in more applications.
- Curriculum offer - in the current financial climate, many schools are struggling to maintain a diverse curriculum that matches expectations. But others who are benefiting from the funding reforms may be able to offer a broad and attractive curriculum.
- Extra-curricular activities - parents often want their children to experience a wide range of activities, either because they have ambitions for a future career in sport, music, creative arts etc, or because the family can't afford to provide the opportunities. Schools which offer these may be more popular.
- New or expanding schools - these can be very hard to compete with if you have a trend of empty places. Not all new free schools are in an area with a shortage of places, and expanding schools are usually already over-subscribed.
- Schools with a different age range - for example, a three-tier system in a neighbouring area when you are a primary or secondary school, or vice versa. Pupils may leave prematurely to start at a middle or high school, or they could finish a middle school then join a secondary school. The challenge is in identifying how many pupils are likely to take this route.

You will be aware of many of these, and your school may be working to address some of them. The benefit of scenario planning is that in these situations, you can use your three options, best, middle and worst, to model some variations.

One last thought: don't assume that all schools will be adversarial about admissions. You may be able to identify a group of headteachers and principals who can see the benefits of working together across an area to prevent the loss of pupils to schools in another locality. While this often happens naturally in multi-academy trusts and faith schools, it can work with any group of schools. If it doesn't exist in your area, why not suggest it?

Other local influences

So far, we've considered pupil numbers in terms of general reasons why pupil numbers might change. Let's look at a couple of specific issues which can also cause variations.

Housing

Changes in local housing can play a part in the number of children and young people in an area, whether they involve clearances or new build developments. Things can appear to move slowly, then suddenly work starts. It can be very difficult to predict how influential the changes will be on pupil numbers, but your LA should be able to provide some information.

Wholesale clearances of old estates, often in town centres, can decimate the population in an area as families move out. Depending on their children's ages, where they move to, and childcare arrangements, to name just three considerations, parents may or may not keep them in their current school.

If there is a new estate planned in your locality, your first challenge is to try to find out the likely timescale for the houses to be occupied. Proposals can take a long time to go through all the planning stages, and there is no guaranteed period for building work to be completed. Depending on the size of the development, construction could be planned in phases over a period of two to three years, for example.

The next question is what type of housing will be built. Will it be attractive to families? Your local authority will also have some intelligence on what proportion of occupiers in a new housing estate come from within the area as opposed to moving from outside it. Parents may decide not to move their children between schools if transport is available.

Housing changes can't be relied upon in forecasting, and you should always be cautious about using them in your projections. Nevertheless, it's worth being aware of them in case they are significant enough to cause a real impact. Your LA could contact you very early in the process if you are likely to be asked to expand, since proposals for new developments have to take into account the impact on schools and funding may be requested from a developer for extra classes or a new school (known as a Section 106 agreement).

Pupil mobility

Does your school have high pupil mobility, with pupils frequently joining and leaving outside of the normal admission dates? Or do the year groups stay fairly intact as they move through the school? This is an important element of your pupil number predictions, but by its very nature, it makes it extremely difficult to achieve reliable forecasts. Scenario planning is particularly helpful here, allowing you to build in three different options for the level of pupil mobility.

There are many different reasons for pupil mobility. The following list suggests just a few.

- Families may move into or out of the area.
- Parents unable to secure their first preference may wait until a place becomes available and then move the child.
- A family's circumstances may change, e.g. childcare arrangements, transport issues, job relocation or a change in rented accommodation, making another school more practical.
- Parental lifestyles may involve frequent movement, e.g. members of the armed forces, travellers, fairground employees etc.
- An area may have a naturally high level of migration, either in or out.
- A village, town, city or region may be designated as a City of Sanctuary for people fleeing violence and persecution, resulting in the sudden arrival of refugees.

We suggest that the best way of tackling this is to build your initial roll projections without taking account of mobility, then apply a turnover allowance, i.e. a percentage change (positive or negative) to each year group. You can vary the rate of turnover to produce the best, middle and worst-case options across the three years.

Parental perceptions

Parental preference may not be an issue if you are a popular school which is usually oversubscribed. But if you are competing for pupils with other schools in your area, and especially if you have surplus places, you will need to consider how significant parental perceptions might be for your future pupil numbers.

We are using the term 'parent' to include carers and anyone who has a say in where a child is educated. Childcare arrangements outside of school hours can be an important influence, so grandparents and other family members might be part of the decision-making process. Where children are already attending education settings, they and their parents may be hearing opinions from teachers and other staff about the suitability of local schools for the next stage.

If you are a primary school, do you have a good relationship with settings such as nurseries, playgroups and childminders? If you are a secondary school, do you foster links with the full range of potential primary 'feeder' schools? Depending on the local admissions policy, you will probably have formal admission links with a smaller subset, but you may want to consider others in the local area, or even beyond it. Schools that are further afield may supply new pupils if transport links are good and your curriculum or pastoral offer is particularly popular.

It's not only formal links with partner schools which are important; other adults who come into contact with a family can convey messages about a school which may or may not be accurate. Are there any community groups in your area where parents and carers gather, and can you make contact with the people who run them to let them know about the quality of your provision?

Running a community facility yourself can allow prospective parents to see what is on offer at your school and feel part of it before they have to make the decision about applying for a place, although the Coronavirus pandemic has interfered with this option rather dramatically.

It's worth trying to come up with a list of potential influences on parents when they are making an application for a school place. Here are just a few, but you will be able to identify others.

- An adverse inspection report can cause a dip in applications and vice versa. A lot hinges on how the result is covered in the local media and how the school handles it.
- Test and exam results can also play a part in parental decisions, but don't overestimate this aspect; you might be surprised how few parents focus on this. My daughter did, but she's a school data technician! Friendships and ease of getting to the school can be seen as more important. But a big drop in results could have an adverse effect on admissions, by making parents less confident about their child's chances if they think it might take some time for the school to achieve improvements.
- A new headteacher can inspire confidence if they start building relationships with the community and parents can see that there is a clear vision and an appealing ethos for the school.
- Parents may have a difference of opinion with their child's teacher or the head and decide to remove their child. Sometimes it can only take a difference of opinion to cause problems, whatever the issue (and it can seem a very small issue to you).
- Parents may feel the school cannot meet the needs of their child, e.g. rejecting a mainstream school in favour of a special school for a pupil with SEND.

In all aspects of parental preference, good public relations can help. It's very competitive out there, so try to get your SLT to work with your council's media team to get good news stories out and show your school in the best possible light.

Key points

- There are many influences on your future rolls. Start with a backwards look at your previous trends in admissions and in-year movement.

- Consider demographic trends. Your local authority will have useful intelligence through its place planning function, and your staff will have knowledge of pupils' younger siblings.
- Think about the competition from other schools and identify the main reasons. Can you do anything about them?
- Changes in housing in the local area and pupil mobility can have an impact on rolls.
- Parental perceptions are important; try to understand how they are formed and where you can develop helpful relationships to maximise the level of applications.

6

PUPIL NUMBER PROJECTIONS

Setting the baseline

The most important fact to remember when dealing with pupil numbers in forecasting is that there is a time lag in the data that is used to calculate your funding for each financial year. Your core funding is based on the October census prior to the financial year being funded, not the pupil numbers actually in school in that year. Please check this carefully, to avoid overstating or understating your total funding across the three years.

This time lag can be beneficial when you have falling rolls, providing a breathing space for you to adjust your expenditure in advance of next year's budget. But it can be a curse when you are growing, as you have to absorb the cost of additional pupils in September until your next budget allocation arrives (unless you qualify for growth funding from the LA to meet basic need). For academies, it's a cost pressure for a whole year.

Structure of the pupil number forecasting model

The first step in creating your model is to set a baseline. This should be the latest year for which you have a funding statement. You must use the rolls on this statement as your baseline.

We recommend that when you create your model, you break down this figure into year groups, especially if you experience pupil mobility. This will allow you to reflect any unusual patterns in individual year groups as they move through the school.

If you are always full, and don't expect any variation across year groups, you can use key stage totals if you wish, but we consider it's better to have the facility to analyse and adjust rolls at year group level, just in case your circumstances change.

The timing of your pupil number forecasts

Depending on the point in the year when you are constructing your pupil number forecasts, the time lag can be helpful. If you are working on your Year 1 forecast after the October census, you will already know your funded pupil numbers for that year.

But bear in mind that until you receive your funding statement, you won't know whether the government's checking process has identified any pupils who have also been claimed by another school. If there is any doubt as to the main registration, the DfE will share the pupil 50:50 between the schools in the data it gives to LAs for use in the local formula.

We'll go into more details on constructing the worksheet in the next chapter. For now, make a very important mental note to focus on the **funded** rolls for each financial year in the model, not the actual pupils you are teaching during that year.

Here's an example which we used when constructing our test model. If you are building your forecasts after October 2020 but before receiving your budget pack for 2021/22, your plan might look like this:

Figure 4: Example of roll forecasting timeline

Forecasting year	Financial year	Census date	Basis of forecast
Baseline	2020/21	Oct 2019	Funding statement
Year 1	2021/22	Oct 2020	Census return submitted, adjusted for possible duplicates
Year 2	2022/23	Oct 2021	Census estimate
Year 3	2023/24	Oct 2022	Census estimate

Later, we'll talk about the impact of pupils starting or leaving in year groups outside the normal times. You'll find out how to adjust your rolled-forward numbers to cater for this. It's important to reflect anything that will affect the next set of census data used for your funding allocation.

Checking your information

Before you start to set up your model, think about what you already know. You may already have financial planning software with roll forecasts in it. How long ago did you prepare them? What assumptions did you make? Are they up to date?

If you are in this situation, now is a good time to review your existing forecasts and consider whether your circumstances have changed. Are there any new influences on your pupil numbers now, or has their impact changed compared to a couple of years ago?

If you haven't done any detailed work on pupil number forecasts, look at the assumptions underpinning your school development plan, curriculum plan or staffing plan. Review them in the light of the four key influences we discussed in chapter 5 – demography, competition, local influences (such as housing and mobility), and parental perceptions – and think about how much of an impact they have on your rolls.

Before setting your year group or key stage rolls, ask yourself what actions you could take to reduce the risks that you've identified. Then make an informed decision about how the rolls might change across the three-year period in your best, middle and worst-case options.

Don't forget to build the time lag into your calculations when you create your estimates, using your funded pupils from the previous October census for each financial year, not the current pupil numbers.

Estimating future pupil numbers is not an exact science. Much of it will be based on intelligence gathered from a range of sources, some of which we've already highlighted. It also needs a large slice of your own judgement. You will probably identify a lot of questions, but you aren't expected to have all the answers; there are many unknown factors.

The point is that being aware of all these issues and spending time discussing them with colleagues will give you a far better chance of making reasonable predictions for the future. However tricky it might seem, it is better to consider the possibilities and prepare for them than to shrug your shoulders and say you can't do anything because it's impossible to tell what might happen.

Pupil number options worksheet

Now it's time to create your first worksheet. Your aim at this stage is to produce best, middle and worst-case options for the pupil numbers that will drive your funding for the next three years.

Activity 2: Creating the roll projections worksheet

- Create a worksheet containing three tables for your best, middle and worst-case roll projections. You need to reflect the breakdown across year groups in the baseline year (funded pupils in the most recent budget statement) and projections for the following three years, preferably for individual year groups, or for key stage totals if you are confident of a stable situation over the full three years. See our primary school best-case example at the foot of this activity.
- If you want to reflect pupil mobility, you can add a line at the foot of the table for each option to apply a turnover allowance (a percentage) to each year group or Key Stage. This lets you adjust your rolls in a transparent and flexible way, including different turnover rates for the three options if you wish.
- Populate the baseline row in the best-case option by entering the year group figures which balance to the total roll on your latest funding statement. Copy this into the middle and worst-case options; these figures won't change.
- Shading the best, middle and worst-case options in different colours will help you avoid errors in a later stage when you start to combine them with per-pupil funding figures.
- Save this as your forecasting file.

Figure 5: Example of roll projections table (best-case)

1. Roll projections - best case scenario										
		Census date	R	Y1	Y2	Y3	Y4	Y5	Y6	R-Y6 total
Baseline	2020/21	Oct-19	44	42	38	44	50	52	51	321
Year 1	2021/22	Oct-20								-
Year 2	2022/23	Oct-21								-
Year 3	2023/24	Oct-22								-
Turnover allowance										

If you would like more details, consult the PDF of our sample model.

* * *

The next activity involves creating formulae to roll forward your pupil numbers across the three-year period and enter a turnover allowance to reflect pupil mobility, if required. You may prefer to enter future estimated rolls manually; if so, remember to make a note of your rationale.

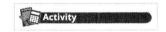

Activity 3: Calculations of pupil projections

- Leave the intake year column of each option blank for now. You'll be entering your admission estimates in Activity 4.
- Depending on the time of year, you may know your latest census figures on which your Year 1 funding will be based. If so, you can enter these in the Year 1 row for all three options. Otherwise, incorporate year 1 in the next step.
- Create formulae to roll forward year groups or key stages to years 2 and 3 and apply the turnover allowance if required. Test it out with some random figures. You may wish to use the ROUND function; if so, please see our note on the PDF.

* * *

The accompanying PDF suggests the formulae you can use for this activity. If you are a middle or high school, you will need to amend the model to reflect the correct intake year.

Populating the worksheet

Choosing different levels of pupil numbers for your best, middle and worst-case options needs careful thought, because later on you'll be multiplying them by your per-pupil funding options. The differences between these options might seem relatively small at this stage, but they will be magnified when you convert them into cash.

There are two ways of reflecting changes in pupil numbers between the best, middle and worst-case options:

- Varying the level of admissions to the intake year.
- Applying a positive or negative turnover allowance to the rolled-forward pupil numbers to reflect the pattern of starters/leavers in years outside of the normal intake year.

Combining these two methods gives a more flexible set of forecasts.

Use the information in chapter 5 to help you decide which factors might be significant for your school. **Don't forget that you are dealing with funded rolls relating to financial years, and therefore the pupil numbers must refer to the October census BEFORE the financial year in question.**

To make it easier to produce your Financial Sustainability Plan, remember to record your debates and the reasons for your choices. It will also help if you need to review your estimates, make adjustments, or if there is a change of finance personnel. It will be easier to identify what has changed and update the figures. Understanding the elements within the projections means that at a later point, you can test them against what actually happened, and refine your planning going forward.

Firming up your assumptions

You will probably come up with a lot of questions, but you aren't expected to have all the answers; there are so many unknown factors. The point is that being aware of all these issues and spending time discussing them with colleagues will give you a far better chance of making reasonable predictions for the future.

Remember that you aren't expected to be accurate, but you are at least trying to achieve a more realistic forecast of the funding likely to come to your school. It can only be broad-brush in nature, but it's much better than not giving any thought at all to the funding part of the equation when compiling your three-year plan.

We can only make suggestions on pupil number forecasting as a starting point; you will know your own circumstances and can judge what the main issues are that you need to look at. Talk to as many people as you can to elicit information and opinions about what the future holds. The art of leadership isn't knowing everything yourself, but knowing who the experts are who can provide reliable information.

The governing body needs to be part of the forward planning process; Ofsted will expect to see their involvement at a strategic level. When there are any leadership changes, it is essential that a new headteacher or Chair of Governors can pick up the projections and quickly get an understanding of the assumptions and the basis on which they have been made.

It's therefore wise to arrange a discussion with your governing body about the patterns of admissions and turnover you have identified and seek their views on what might change in the future. You may be lucky enough to have governors with their finger on the pulse of the community or with knowledge of areas that you've identified as affecting your admissions. They may be able to provide further information to add to the mix.

It is your call as to how much weight you attach to each piece of information. Be sure to ask the following questions before using it as a basis for your assumptions:

- Is it evidenced?
- Is it reasonably reliable?
- Is it likely to influence the number of children who may come to your school in the future?

In the next activity, you will complete the roll projections by entering estimated admissions and turnover allowances as appropriate to your situation.

Activity 4: Estimating admissions and turnover

- Using our guidance, enter the estimated admissions figures for your intake year in the September immediately before the relevant October census for funded rolls (actuals in Year 1 if you know them). In our example, for Y2, the 2022/23 financial year, this would be pupils admitted in September 2021.
- If your school experiences pupil mobility, enter appropriate turnover percentages in the relevant row for each option to adjust the rolled-forward figures. You can add more sensitivity to your forecasts if desired by varying the turnover rate across the best, middle and worst-case options.
- Review the results and make any adjustments you consider necessary to achieve a reasonable set of options.

You can consult the PDF to see a completed version.

* * *

Agreeing the assumptions

Having thought about the different influences on your admissions and the progression of pupils through the school, you may be keen to move to the next stage of creating the model. But it's important to discuss your assumptions with your colleagues in SLT and governors and record the debate. This will save time later if there is a change in any of the key players and/or anyone queries the decisions.

Holding these discussions at each stage of building the model will help you to gain the confidence of your colleagues and governors and secure their commitment to the process. When you start to bring all the different elements together in your final scenarios, you will have created a deeper understanding of the issues. Everyone will be aware of the potential for external events to cause disruption, and expectations of accuracy will be tempered.

Using estimates of future rolls within the model will help to improve your financial planning in times of pupil roll uncertainty. The use of scenarios helps to illustrate this, by allowing for a range of possibilities to be tested.

You might feel that if your pupil number variations are quite limited, they won't have much impact. But once you combine them with different options for per-pupil funding, it can open everyone's eyes to the potential for turbulence in the school's future funding allocations. Your work may also be used to inform future curriculum design and staffing plans.

Well done for completing the pupil number element of your core funding scenarios. We will now move on to some background information on the funding system to help you understand the context for your per-pupil funding forecasts.

Key points

- Set your baseline for pupil numbers, based on **funded pupils** for the current financial year, i.e. those on your funding statement.
- If you know the census data in the October prior to your year 1 forecast, you can use it, but allow for possible duplicate pupils.
- Create a pupil number options worksheet for the three options across the three-year period, rolling forward year groups and adjusting them using a turnover allowance if mobility is a feature.
- Estimate the level of admissions in each year.
- Get agreement for your assumptions and record the rationale to use in your Financial Sustainability Plan.

7

THE CONTEXT FOR PER-PUPIL FUNDING

Forecasting pupil-led funding

The next part of the process deals with pupil-led funding, by which we mean the main factors within school budget share for LA maintained schools or the equivalent allocation in the first line of academy GAG statements. The factors involved are mainly those which relate to pupil characteristics; the term the DfE uses for them is 'pupil-led funding'. You'll have the chance to estimate the remaining factors and other sources of funding in the later stages of building your model.

Estimating pupil-led funding is more technically challenging than your work on pupil numbers, but we'll show you how to pick up important clues from the available information. As you will be rolling forward the model beyond the initial three years, knowing a little about the funding system will help you to understand and interpret future government decisions for forecasting purposes. We will guide you through all of this.

As we mentioned in chapter 1, there are two main influences on your funding levels: the national total allocated to schools and how it's distributed between them. Let's look first at the total funding provided for schools.

Level of funding for schools

The decision-making process for school funding at a national level involves the Treasury setting out the government's spending plans for the public sector. This exercise is called a Spending Review. The period covered by the settlement can vary, but three years is fairly common.

In 2019, due to the difficulties over Brexit, a one-year Spending Review took place, setting out 2020/21 spending plans for most government departments. But exceptionally, due to sustained lobbying about the state of health and school budgets, the Chancellor announced a five-year settlement for the NHS and a three-year settlement for education covering the period 2020/21 to 2022/23.

In 2020, a three-year review was planned for the remaining departments, but in October 2020 the Chancellor announced it would be again be limited to a one-year review, to determine budgets for 2021/22.

The multi-year education settlement provided a total increase of £7.1 billion by 2022/23 compared to 2019/20 for the Dedicated Schools Grant (DSG). This grant is paid to LAs, and it includes the Schools Block which they then have to distribute among local schools. The increase was phased across the three years: an extra £2.6 billion in 2020/21, another £2.2bn in 2021/22 and a further £2.3bn in 2022/23. But there the detail ends; the distribution of the money is announced individually for each year under the normal budgeting process.

This additional funding has to cover both the Schools and High Needs blocks. In 2020/21, £780m of the £2.6bn increase went to the High Needs Block, followed by another £730m in 2021/22. The outcome of the government's review of the system for supporting pupils with SEND won't make any difference to funding until 2022/23, unless a magic money tree is found before then!

If you want to know more about what the settlement means for the school sector, i.e. what cost pressures it needs to cover, you can read a helpful article by the Education Policy Institute at https://epi.org.uk/publications-and-research/spending-round-preview/. This dates from September 2019, when the settlement was announced.

. . .

Affordability of pay awards

Each year, the Secretary of State gives evidence to the School Teachers' Review Body (STRB) about the financial context for the annual pay award for teachers. The government refused to provide a grant to cover the September 2020 pay award, saying the additional funding in the settlement would cover it. But this is a misguided view, because as we'll see shortly, not all schools will receive the full increase.

While the current funding for pay and pensions increases will continue, it's important to note that this **only covers the September 2018 and 2019 awards**. Schools will therefore need to find the money for the 2020 award. This may be extremely difficult for many, especially those who spend a high proportion of their budget on teaching staff or who have a lot of early career teachers receiving the higher percentage increases under the new arrangements. It seems ironic, after years of being told to replace upper scale leavers with lower cost teachers to make savings!

One development which you will need to build into your forecasts is the decision to transfer the pay and pensions grants into the National Funding Formula from 2021/22. We will explain this further in the section on how funding is distributed.

What this means for forecasting

Knowing the pattern of funding settlements provides some boundaries for your estimates of per-pupil funding. Taking the current settlement as an example, if year 3 of your forecasts falls after 2022/23, you will have absolutely no idea whether the government's plans for schools involve cuts, a modest increase which only covers unavoidable cost pressures (also known as a real-terms freeze), or higher investment-style increases in the national total.

This suggests a need to be very cautious in estimates for 2023/24 and beyond, until the government provides more information. But since you're compiling three options for your per-pupil funding, you at least have the potential to explore the possibilities.

However, there is an important caveat: while the settlement gives you a high-level indication of the potential course of school funding at the national level, it doesn't necessarily help you to decide how your school will fare. The next area to consider is how the funding is distributed.

Distribution of funding

For a very long time, historic inequalities in school funding have been a concern, but progress in sorting them out has been extremely slow. By the time the National Funding Formula (NFF) was introduced in 2018/19, austerity measures meant the government couldn't afford to level up the allocations so that all schools with the same characteristics received the higher levels of funding allocated in some parts of the country.

The initial plans for the NFF therefore removed money from those with high levels of funding and gave it to those regarded as previously underfunded.

This period also saw significant unfunded cost pressures, and the combination of the two issues led to school funding gaining a high profile in the 2017 General Election campaign. As a result, more money was found for the NFF when it was introduced in 2018/19, so that schools who were on a downward trajectory in the pure formula could at least receive a positive increase per pupil, however minimal, rather than an actual loss.

The aim is still to reduce these schools' funding down to the NFF level, but it will now take much longer. The graph below shows the trajectory in per-pupil funding if the current increases were to continue.

Figure 6: Theoretical trajectory to pure National Funding Formula

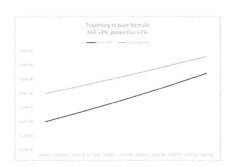

The issue is that the inflation levels applied to the NFF factors are quite low, creating a fairly narrow gap between the increase given to schools on the NFF and the level of protection paid to those above it.

The grey line on our illustrative graph depicts a theoretical school starting at a notional £6,000 per pupil and receiving protection against NFF losses should the 2021/22 minimum uplift of 2% per year continue.

The black line is the NFF result for another theoretical school with the same characteristics funded at £5,000 per pupil with an increase of 3% per year, assuming the 2021/22 uplift continues. The overall NFF has gone up by 4%, but some of this has been used to fund increases in pupils/charac-teristics data and schools qualifying for protection.

You can see that if this pattern continued, the gap would narrow, but even after ten years, the funding levels for the two schools remain a good distance apart. There are two ways in which the allocations could converge sooner: if protection were reduced and/or if the pure NFF values were increased further.

If you are an academy within a multi academy trust which practises GAG pooling, as described in chapter 2, please remember that you might not receive the NFF values even under the Hard NFF. A minority of trusts currently practise pooling, but interest in it has grown as deficits become a bigger issue. If you have autonomy over finance and wish to create funding forecasts, talk to your trust to establish whether it's part of their future plans. It may not be fruitful to even attempt forecasts if the trust is likely to redistribute funding.

Phasing of the NFF

When a government is changing the distribution of funding via a national formula, there will inevitably be tensions between accuracy and simplicity. The more accurately you try to reflect the need to spend, the more complex the formula will be. Conversely, if you try to keep it simple, it becomes more difficult to account for different types of need.

The rate at which schools moved towards the NFF therefore became a big issue during its early implementation. The DfE decided it would be best to let local authorities manage the initial transition and give schools time to adapt, by shifting local formulae towards the NFF gradually, before it was imposed on everyone.

This resulted in a plan to introduce the NFF in two stages: a 'Soft NFF' followed by a 'Hard NFF'. The distinction between the two stages is important for your forecasting, because it determines whether or not you need to take into account any local decisions. Understanding these two stages will make it easier to follow our guidance later.

The Soft NFF

Under the Soft NFF, the DfE establishes values for all the factors in the National Funding Formula and uses these to calculate Schools Block allocations of Dedicated Schools Grant (DSG) to local authorities. LAs then distribute the money between schools using a local formula, as under the previous system. At the time of writing, we know this system will remain in place until the end of 2021/22 at least.

The local formula continues to be the basis for GAG allocations to academies while the Soft NFF is in place. The LA calculates a budget share for them and includes the allocations in its annual return, then the DfE claws back the money so that ESFA can make the payments to trusts.

There are some restrictions on an LA's freedom within the local arrangements, especially in relation to transitional protection, which we'll explain later. LA decisions on the pace at which the local formula moves towards the NFF values have to be undertaken in close consultation with their schools. These decisions partly depend on the starting point (the historic formula), local priorities, and how much money the LA receives in the grant allocations. The last of these has become a crucial issue as cost pressures have increased.

The importance of the Soft NFF for your forecasting is that while it is in place, your estimates of per-pupil funding will need to anticipate the decisions your local authority will take on the local formula.

Most LAs have already adopted the NFF or seem to be working towards it, so this aspect is getting progressively easier to predict for many schools. But local circumstances might make it difficult for LAs to replicate the NFF exactly in any given year even if they want to, as we'll explain shortly. It's therefore important to keep in touch with what your LA is intending to do.

You can do this by viewing your area's Schools Forum papers, which should be on a public-facing website; the budget strategy is usually agreed in the autumn term. You can ask your Forum representatives for updates, or you could attend meetings as an observer, which can also be good professional development.

It's worth understanding how the grant is calculated under the Soft NFF, to help you interpret the available information for your forecasting exercise. There are two elements to the grant calculation, school-level and LA-level; we'll take the school-level element first.

School-level allocations within the NFF

The calculation of LA Schools Block grant is done in two stages: an initial provisional set of allocations, usually published at the end of the summer term (the 2021/22 information appeared in July 2020), then a final grant calculation in December.

The purpose of the provisional allocations is for DfE to fix a 'unit of funding' (a per-pupil amount) for each primary and secondary pupil. This will form the basis of the grant paid to each LA in the following year; an early decision allows local authorities to do some early planning.

The downside of this system is that the calculation can only be based on the pupil numbers that are available at the time, i.e. the previous October's school census. For the provisional 2021/22 allocations, the data goes back to October 2019. The upside is that the provisional information includes figures for individual schools, suggesting the likely trajectory for your per-pupil funding according to the NFF.

But there are three important caveats:

- the figures don't reflect the actual rolls which will be used to distribute the funding for the financial year in question;
- they don't include growth funding and other non-NFF elements (see LA-level allocations below);
- your LA might not deliver the NFF in the local formula under the Soft NFF.

The reason for the first of these is that the **final LA grant** is calculated by multiplying the units of funding by the **new census data**, e.g. October

2020 for 2021/2022. The updated pupil numbers are also used for the local formula.

You must therefore ignore the cash amounts in the provisional allocations. But as we'll see, you can use the per-pupil funding change for your forecasts.

LA-level allocations

There is another part of the Schools Block grant allocation to the LA which is not at school level and sits outside the NFF. This involves factors which are difficult to distribute via a formula, such as Private Finance Initiative costs, non-domestic rates and some exceptional circumstances funding such as dual use, rents, and unusual premises features. The majority of them are set at the amount the LA planned to spend in the previous year; you may see them referred to as historic spend factors.

These issues are part of the reason why it's taking a while to move to the second stage of a Hard NFF. The DfE can't handle individual school circumstances, and there are some significant technical challenges in finding appropriate mechanisms to distribute the money. Imagine if a PFI school suddenly saw a reduction in its funding for meeting contractual obligations!

Growth funding

Funding for pupil number growth is also allocated at LA level, because the DfE doesn't know which schools will qualify in the next financial year. Growth funding allocations to LAs are based on the change in rolls between the last two October censuses (2019 and 2020 for the financial year 2021/22). They aren't included in the provisional allocations at all, because the DfE wants to minimise the time lag. The Department therefore waits until the new census data is available and announces the growth amounts as part of the actual DSG allocations in December. LAs are given a tool in advance of this, to help them to estimate it.

There is the potential for a cost pressure due to this one-year time lag in data, because the funding is a year out of date by the time the LA has to assess eligibility and make the payments to qualifying schools for new classes in the following September. The LA has to manage this tension from within the overall Schools Block allocation.

Tensions in the local formula

We mentioned earlier that LAs might find it difficult to replicate the NFF locally, even if they want to. Here are a few reasons why this might be the case in your area:

- The updated census data may require more money in local formula factors such as deprivation, low prior attainment and English as an Additional Language. This won't be reflected in the units of funding within the LA's grant, which are based on pupil profiles from the year before.
- Allocations based on historic spend, such as rates and pupil number growth, may not be sufficient for the financial year in question, causing a pressure which has to be managed within the grant. PFI is the exception, in that it receives a national inflationary uplift, but it may not be enough to cover the contractual increase for schools in the local area.
- Funding for SEND is in crisis, with many LAs seeing increasing deficits. LAs are allowed to transfer up to 0.5% of their annual Schools Block allocation to the High Needs Budget, as long as the Schools Forum gives its approval. This reduces the amount of money available in the formula for mainstream schools. LAs can appeal to the Secretary of State if the Forum refuses, or they can ask for permission to transfer more than 0.5% with the Forum's agreement. If you want to know more about this, Julie's blog post highlights the gap between SEND funding and costs: https://schoolfinancialsuccess.com/the-invisible-send-review/.

You can see why it's taking a while for the government to commit to a Hard NFF; they have to resolve all of these issues before they can bring everything into a formulaic approach.

The Hard NFF

Under the Hard NFF, the DFE will still calculate allocations for individual schools using the national formula, but will then fund every school and academy in the country directly, using the NFF values. There will no longer be a local formula in each area.

The timescale for a move to the Hard NFF is uncertain, but the announcements for 2021/22 brought a confirmation that it can't happen before 2022/23. Direct funding of all schools by DfE (the Hard NFF) requires primary legislation, so as the Parliamentary timetable develops during 2021, there should be some signs to indicate whether it's likely to happen in 2022/23 or whether it will be delayed again. You can be sure that Julie will be keeping an eye on it and reporting in the newsletter and blog on any developments, including any opportunities for consultation responses.

As well as the technical difficulties mentioned in the previous section, there is a big question mark over how funding for SEND can be managed under the Hard NFF, given that it offers no prospect of any flexibility to move money between the Schools and High Needs blocks. If LAs have to rely solely on the High Needs Block allocation, the onus will be on the DfE to provide enough money so that pupils with SEND and those in alternative provision and hospital education settings can receive the support they need. That's not an attractive proposition for Ministers.

The Hard NFF could also cause a substantial increase in demand on the ESFA's capacity, as the number of mainstream schools they will have to deal with will rise from around 8,700 (the number of academies at August 2020) to a total of over 20,600 including LA primary and secondary schools. Special schools and AP settings will still be funded from the LA's High Needs Budget (with money recovered from LAs by ESFA for academies).

Protection mechanisms for those adversely affected by the NFF have played an important role in avoiding disastrous funding reductions for individual schools. The details of the protection levels can play an important role in your forecasting if your current funding is higher than the NFF values, so let's take a little time to explore them.

Protections against losses

There are two main types of protection within the calculation of each LA's grant for schools. The aim is to reduce the risks to schools who would see much lower levels of funding if the pure NFF were imposed. The protection arrangements can be used to set your worst-case option, as they are literally the lowest permissible level of per-pupil funding.

We'll now explain the two methods of protection. One provides an absolute value per pupil and the other ensures a minimum percentage increase in per-pupil funding. You could qualify for both, but for most schools disadvantaged by the NFF, it's more likely to be one or the other.

Minimum Per Pupil Levels (MPPL)

MPPLs are meant to provide a realistic amount of funding per pupil for the lowest funded schools, usually those with minimal additional needs. The amounts are confirmed each year and there are separate values for each key stage, enabling different calculations for primary, middle, secondary and high schools.

For primary schools, it's a straightforward single cash total per pupil. For others, the minimum level is a weighted average based on the number of year groups in the relevant key stages. If the pure NFF doesn't provide this level of per-pupil funding, the LA is awarded an extra amount to allow the school to reach it.

Some people have erroneously assumed the MPPL values are based on the Age Weighted Pupil Unit (AWPU) factor (also called basic entitlement). That would be nice for the schools concerned, but sadly it isn't true! The MPPL value includes all factors relating to pupil numbers and characteristics, plus the lump sum and sparsity allocations. The factors which are excluded from the calculation are pupil number growth, premises items and exceptional circumstances funding.

Your LA must pass on the MPPLs in the local formula to qualifying schools; they have no choice. If you are a school in this position, you can therefore use this as the first test to establish your worst-case option for per-pupil funding levels in cash terms.

. . .

Funding floor/Minimum Funding Guarantee (MFG)

Whereas the MPPLs deal with cash amounts, the second layer of protection, the MFG, relates to the percentage change in per-pupil funding each year. There are two versions of it, national and local. When the DfE applies it to the LA grant calculation it's known as the funding floor, and when the LA uses it in the local formula it's called the Minimum Funding Guarantee (MFG). As we'll see, the level of protection can differ between the two under the Soft NFF.

This protection prevents individual schools from experiencing large percentage reductions in per-pupil funding from one year to the next as a result of the NFF. It provides a guaranteed percentage increase in funding per pupil, which is decided annually.

When the NFF was first introduced in 2018/19, the funding floor protection applied to the individual school calculations within the LA grant was set at a minimum increase of 1% in total across the first two years. In 2020/21 it was set at +1.84% and in 2021/22 it is +2%.

The calculation for both the funding floor and MFG differs slightly from the MPPL calculation. It measures the change in total **pupil-led** funding. The difference is that it excludes the lump sum and sparsity allocations. As with the MPPL, pupil number growth, premises items and exceptional circumstances funding are also excluded.

However, the MFG that schools actually receive can be lower than the funding floor, because LAs have some discretion over the MFG. This recognises that for the reasons we've already noted, authorities may be unable to balance the formula to the available grant.

But the LA's options are limited; they must choose a MFG increase within a range set by the government. In 2020/21 and 2021/22, the lowest possible MFG is an increase of +0.5% per pupil and the highest is the NFF funding floor level for the year in question (+1.84% and +2% respectively).

Transfer of pay and pensions grants into the NFF

In 2021/22, the existing separate pay and pensions grants received in 2020/21 will be transferred into the NFF pot. DfE has made clear its intention in the guidance on these grants:

'We have ensured that the additional funding schools will attract through the NFF is as close as possible to the funding they would have received if the funding was continuing as separate grants, without adding significant complexity to the formulae.'

Note the use of the word 'attract'. This word usually refers to the money the DfE gives to LAs for each school, with the unspoken (and often overlooked) caveat that it might not be replicated in the local formula.

Fortunately, there's a strong likelihood that most schools will see the continuation of their current pay and pensions grants from 2021/22 onwards. Elements which were originally allocated on pure pupil numbers (all of the pay grant and the basic part of the pensions grant) will be transferred into the AWPU factor, so you should see an increase in that unit value (subject to LA decisions in the Soft NFF). The Supplementary Fund for the teachers' pension increase grant will be allocated separately; those with high levels of deprivation and SEND are likely to qualify for it.

The grant transfers are guaranteed if you qualify for protection:

- The MPPLs for 2021/22 are being increased to reflect the grant transfers (an extra £180 per primary pupil and £265 per secondary pupil)
- The baseline for the LA's MFG calculation for each school must be increased by the value of the grants received in 2020/21.

But please remember that the grant transfer only relates to funding provided for the September 2018 and 2019 teachers' pay award. At the time of writing, there is no extra money for the September 2020 award.

Using the protection in forecasting

You can use these protections to establish your worst-case options for per-pupil funding across the three years of your funding forecasts. Even if you are seeing an increase in the national provisional amounts (we'll show you where to find this later), your LA may not be able to afford to give you the full increase, so it's best to allow for the minimum levels in your worst-case option.

Limits on gains

The NFF was introduced at a time when there was very little extra money for education. But the protections outlined above created a significant cost pressure. Given the political imperative to avoid huge losses for individual schools, which could pose a risk to pupil outcomes, the only way of affording this was to limit gains for schools which were previously underfunded.

To achieve this, a system known as capping was introduced. This involved making an adjustment to reduce very high gains, freeing up some money to fund protection. This was called capping, and it helped the DfE to balance the formula to the available resources.

Capping was not popular, because it meant that schools which needed a big increase had to wait longer for it. But with no extra funding made available, there was no other option at the time. LAs were also allowed to cap gains in the local formula, in order to meet the cost of protection.

The situation has shifted slightly since more money was found in the settlement from 2020/21 onwards. As well as covering rising rolls and (some) inflationary pressures, the extra funding has been used to abolish capping in the calculation of LA grant. This means that **in theory,** the funding provided to LAs is sufficient to allow all schools below the NFF to move straight on to it.

However, as explained earlier, even if an LA wants to adopt the NFF, there might be local circumstances which make it difficult to replicate the national formula within the available resources. Capping of gains is therefore still permitted in the local formula if required. This could change, so watch out for it while the Soft NFF is still in place.

If an LA practises capping, it must not take a school below the minimum per pupil funding level (MPPL). Capping also cannot be applied to schools that have opened in the last seven years and have not reached their full number of year groups.

What does this mean for forecasting?

If you are gaining from the NFF, when you compile forecasts under the Soft NFF you need to find out whether your LA is planning to cap gains in order to balance the formula. This is likely to be a late decision, after the LA receives its DSG allocation in December, so your best bet may be to look back at previous years. If it's been normal practice, it's safest to build it into your options, although you may have to guess the maximum percentage gain that the LA will allow. You can update your model when the LA consults on proposals and communicates its decisions.

In the next chapter, you'll discover the key information that will guide your assumptions for the per-pupil funding part of your model.

Key points

- Understanding the school funding system will help you interpret future policy changes when rolling forward forecasts.
- Government Spending Reviews determine the national total available for schools, but the distribution of funding depends on the National Funding Formula.
- You need to make assumptions on when the Soft NFF (with LA funding formulae) will end and when the Hard NFF (direct funding from the DfE) will be introduced.
- Protection mechanisms can be used for the worst-case scenario.

8

PER-PUPIL FUNDING ASSUMPTIONS

Where to find the information

You can find information to help you develop per-pupil funding options at both a national and local level. Your LA may provide helpful intelligence, but if not, don't despair; we will offer some ideas.

High-level information

The DFE publishes a policy paper each year outlining the main features of the school funding system for the following year. You don't need to read it all; you can focus on key aspects such as the percentage uplift in the NFF factors, any change in the funding floor, the range within which the LA has to set their Minimum Funding Guarantee, and the level of the MPPLs if applicable. The document is relatively clear and accessible; the technical aspects are published separately.

You should be able to find the most current policy paper, 'The national funding formulae for schools and high needs', via this link:

https://www.gov.uk/government/publications/national-funding-formula-for-schools-and-high-needs.

.   .   .

Provisional allocations file

As mentioned earlier, there are some caveats to the school-level provisional school funding allocations: they don't use the rolls on which your funding will actually be based, and the local formula may be different. But they do provide the annual percentage change in per-pupil funding which would apply if you were on the NFF, which is a useful starting point.

The file you need is 'The impact of the Schools NFF'. The link for the 2021/22 file is at: https://www.gov.uk/government/publications/national-funding-formula-tables-for-schools-and-high-needs-2021-to-2022.

For future years, you can search for 'National funding formula tables for schools and high needs' plus the relevant year. Please make sure you select the correct file; it may not be the first one.

Very small schools might not appear in the file; the DfE excludes any where anomalies occur, such as the lump sum being a high proportion of the total, rendering per-pupil funding less meaningful.

Identifying your per-pupil funding change

Figure 7: Example of provisional NFF allocations table

Notional impact of the NFF for the selected school		
2019-20 pupil count	1,169	This is the number of pupils that were in the school in 2019-20, excluding any reception uplift calculated by the local authority.
Baseline funding (2020-21)	£7,474,052	This is a school's 2020-21 NFF allocation, adjusted to reflect the proportion of the year the school is open in 2020-21, and to include funding due to the Teachers' Pay Grant (TPG), the Teachers' Pension Employer Contribution Grant (TPECG) and, if applicable, the pensions supplementary fund.
2020-21 pupil count	1,173	This is the number of pupils that were in the school in 2020-21, excluding any reception uplift calculated by the local authority.
Notional total NFF funding in 2021-22	£7,646,492	This is the amount the department will allocate to local authorities in respect of the school in 2021-22, subject to pupil number changes. The actual amount the school will receive will be determined by the local authority.
Notional total NFF funding in 2021-22 (£ per pupil)	£6,519	This is the notional total NFF funding in 2021-22, divided by the school's 2020-21 pupil numbers.
Percentage change compared to baseline (total)	2.31%	This is the percentage difference between the school's total notional NFF funding in 2021-22 and their baseline funding, as described above. To note, this will also reflect changes in pupil numbers.
Percentage change in pupil-led funding (per pupil)	2.00%	This is the percentage difference between the school's pupil-led funding within their illustrative NFF funding in 2021-22 and the school's pupil-led funding within their baseline. Baseline pupil-led funding includes basic per-pupil funding, additional needs funding, funding due to teachers' pay and pensions grants, and the difference between the school's 2020-21 NFF lump sum/sparsity and the school's 2021-22 NFF lump sum/sparsity. Schools and local authorities can see a detailed explanation of the calculation behind this figure in the COLLECT system.

On opening the file, go to the tab 'Look up a school' and from the dropdown menu, select your local authority and find your school. You can ignore the cash amounts and the line labelled 'percentage change compared to baseline (total)' in this table, because of the time lag in rolls.

Focus on the last line: the percentage change in pupil-led funding. In our example, this is the per-pupil funding change for year 1 (2021/22) if you were on the NFF. The 2% figure in this example is calculated by comparing the 2020/21 baseline pupil-led figure, i.e. £7,474,052 divided by 1,169 pupils (£6,394), with the 2021/22 pupil-led funding of £6,519.

We'll provide guidance on interpreting this table shortly. For now, just make a note of your pupil-led percentage change and save the file with your school selected in case you want to refer to it again later.

Local authority information

In the Soft NFF phase, you need to pick up clues about your LA's intentions for the local formula during the budget setting process. The LA has the final say over it, but it must consult schools on substantial changes. It's worth knowing how your LA approaches budget preparation, to know when information will be available. Here's a guide to the process:

1. Your LA may have a formula working group with school members to work up proposals for change. Its findings should be reported to the Schools Forum, and minutes may be available. This may result in a consultation.
2. Once the DfE provides provisional allocations, the LA produces an initial forecast of its DSG for the following year, multiplying the units of funding by estimated pupil numbers for the next October census. Academies may be asked for estimated rolls; cooperation will make forecasts realistic.
3. The DSG estimate will form the basis of initial budget strategy reports to the Schools Forum in the autumn term. Provisional totals will be identified for the formula (Schools Block), Early Years, High Needs and Central School Services blocks.
4. By early November, the LA may need to ask the Schools Forum to approve transfers from the Schools Block to fund

High Needs pressures. LAs can appeal against a refusal to transfer up to 0.5%. They have to request Ministerial approval for a transfer above 0.5%, even if a Schools Forum approves it.

5. The LA should also request approval from LA school members of the Forum for Central School Services Block (CSSB) spending. If any of the services previously funded from this block cease, the money can be transferred into the formula or be used to cover High Needs pressures. However, the DfE is reducing CSSB allocations, so surpluses are less likely.

6. The LA can also apply unspent balances from previous years to the local formula if available. These will have come from central budgets funded by DSG and will be **one-off** additions; you can't assume the extra money will continue in later years.

7. This all produces an estimated Schools Block total. The LA may present some initial modelling of the funding formula to the Schools Forum along with the results of any consultation. This stage provides important information, such as proposed factor values, the level of protection which may be available, and whether gains will need to be capped or not.

8. Once the DfE has provided a) the new October census dataset for use in the local formula and b) the final DSG allocations, the LA will re-run the modelling. There is a very short timescale for this, as the grant allocations come out just before Christmas, but the formula has to be agreed in January.

9. At the January Forum meeting, the LA presents the proposed formula; it may or may not include school-level allocations.

10. The LA submits a proforma to the DfE in the third week of January. This contains all the funding formula calculations for LA maintained schools and academies.

11. Political approval has to be sought for the formula. The DfE allows this to take place before or after the proforma is submitted, given the tight timescales.

12. The LA has to send budget share allocations to schools at least four weeks before the start of the new financial year. The ESFA usually provides academy allocations later, as they are paid on a September to August financial year.

The Schools Forum is an important conduit for information, and your representatives should keep you informed. You can attend the meetings as an observer, or you could read the papers on the Schools Forum website. LA officers may also do briefings for school leaders and governors.

Whilst there has always been a requirement on LAs to consult on important changes to the local formula, at the time of writing there has been no word from DfE about any arrangements for national consultation with schools on future changes after the Hard NFF is introduced.

If you sign up for Julie's free newsletter, you will receive a monthly update on government announcements relating to finance and funding.

Setting the baseline

There are two stages to building your per-pupil funding options: create a baseline from your current allocation, then decide on different percentage changes for your best, middle and worst-case options.

The timing of the Hard NFF

As with pupil number options, the baseline is set using your most recent funding statement. Due to the uncertain timing of the Hard NFF, it's tricky to know what you can reliably assume. But we need to start somewhere. Below you can see our assumptions, but you can continue to base your forecasts on the LA formula if the Hard NFF is delayed again.

Figure 8: Example timeline for assumptions on Soft and Hard NFF

Forecasting year	Financial year	Basis of forecast
Baseline	2020/21	Funding statement
Year 1	2021/22	Soft NFF - LA formula
Year 2	2022/23	Hard NFF - national formula
Year 3	2023/24	Hard NFF - national formula

Setting your per-pupil funding baseline

The definition of per-pupil funding within your core funding doesn't include every element of budget share. You therefore need to calculate your baseline on the same basis as the DfE's pupil-led allocations. You will add back any excluded items later. In the model, we refer to 'MFG exclusions', since they follow the Minimum Funding Guarantee method.

Activity 5: Setting the per-pupil funding baseline

- In your Excel forecasting file, create a per-pupil funding options worksheet with the description and amount for each item in the baseline calculation which follows. You'll be building on this later for the future year forecasts. Our example worksheet looks like this:

Figure 9: Baseline per-pupil funding calculation

Item		2020/21
		£
1	School's budget share/GAG in baseline year (after MFG and capping but before deducting LA school de-delegation or MAT top slice)	1,350,020
2	Baseline year rates (academies ignore: GAG already excludes)	12,460
2	Baseline year lump sum and sparsity factors	114,400
2	Baseline year additional lump sum for amalgamating schools	0
2	Agreed MFG exclusions and technical adjustments	0
	Total of excluded items	126,860
3	Pay grant received in baseline year	15,931
3	Pension grant received in baseline year	70,635
	Total additions	86,566
	Total baseline (budget share/GAG less exclusions plus additions)	1,309,726
	Funded number on roll from baseline year statement (excluding reception uplift where used)	321
	Baseline funding amount per pupil	£ 4,080.14

- Item 1: Enter your total budget share from your funding statement or the equivalent in your academy GAG statement. This should only relate to pupils in Reception to Y11.
- Check that the figure you are using is your funding allocation

before any adjustments for de-delegation (LA schools), MAT top slice (academies) or subscription to the DfE's Risk Protection Arrangement (RPA). You should also ignore any exclusions adjustments shown on your funding statement.

- Do not include any other items such as nursery, post-16, pupil number growth or SEN top-up funding.
- Item 2: Enter the amounts on your detailed list of formula factors which are excluded items, i.e. not pupil-led: rates (LA maintained schools only), lump sum, sparsity, PFI, and any additional lump sum paid for the first year of an amalgamation. You will deduct these from your budget share. Academies can ignore rates; they aren't in the budget share figure.
- Item 3: If your baseline year is 2020/21, record the pay and pensions grants received in that financial year. You will be adding these amounts to the calculation.
- Create a formula to calculate the total baseline: total budget share before adjustments, less the Item 2 excluded amounts, plus the Item 3 grant transfers if your baseline is 2020/21.
- Divide the new total by the **funded number on roll from your funding statement**, excluding any reception class uplift.

* * *

This will produce your baseline for the per-pupil element of your forecasts. It's important to check its accuracy, as any slight error will be magnified once you start multiplying the forecasts by your pupil number estimates. The PDF shows an example of the baseline table.

Questions to ask

It's time to start thinking about the percentage changes in your per-pupil funding in years 1, 2 and 3. In chapter 7, you improved your understanding of the main issues which might have an impact on your funding. Now you can convert this knowledge into a set of options.

Here is a summary of the questions you need to ask. Just make notes on your answers for now; you'll apply them to your model shortly.

. . .

Question 1: The LA's approach to the NFF

This is a high-level question which you should explore first. What is your LA's policy on moving towards the NFF during the Soft NFF phase? They may have already replicated it, which simplifies things; you can have more confidence in the national provisional allocations.

However, it's important to double check this; the LA may have some difficulty in balancing the local formula to the grant. The best-laid plans can go awry if a lack of funding gets in the way!

If your local formula isn't already delivering the NFF, have officers and politicians signalled an intention to move towards it in stages, and if so, how quickly will it happen? They will hopefully have a clear policy outlining the planned movement in the formula until the NFF is reached (or the Hard NFF is imposed), although planning admittedly becomes more difficult when the government keeps shifting the goalposts.

Alternatively, your LA might be one of the minority who maintain the historic formula, either as a matter of principle or because they want to minimise the local impact of the NFF while they can. One common issue is that the NFF may change the balance of funding between primary and secondary phases in a local area, which can be difficult to manage.

However, as successive annual grants are fixed using the NFF, avoiding it in the local formula could be progressively more difficult to achieve within the available resources. This means the proportion of LAs using the NFF will probably continue to rise during the Soft NFF period.

Question 2: Are transfers to the High Needs Budget likely?

Are there severe pressures in your LA's High Needs Budget? Many LAs have accumulated deficits due to funding not keeping pace with cost pressures, as already mentioned. While reviews have been undertaken at the request of the DfE in an attempt to find savings, High Needs funding continues to fall short, due to increases in both the level of need and costs.

Schools Forums have varying attitudes towards this issue. Some will recognise that without a transfer from the Schools Block, the LA will have to cut payments and services from the High Needs Budget. If savings have to be found, those most adversely affected will be special schools, alternative provision and those mainstream schools which are educating high numbers of pupils with SEND. A transfer spreads the pressure more evenly across all types of school and avoids intensifying the existing disincentives to be exclusive.

On the other hand, some Schools Forums will refuse a request to transfer money and accept that the most inclusive schools will have to absorb more of the costs of SEND support to meet pupils' needs.

Keeping an eye on the LA's proposals will help you decide whether you need to temper your forecasts to allow for a transfer. If one is agreed, the LA may not be able to deliver the NFF levels of funding. The government now prevents LAs from writing off High Needs deficits using council reserves, so all the pressure sits within the overall DSG.

Question 3: Are you gaining or losing from the NFF?

Your decisions on the percentage changes in years 1, 2 and 3 for your three options will be heavily influenced by this question: whether you are benefiting from the NFF, or seeing a real-terms reduction, i.e. a relatively low increase which is unlikely to cover pay awards and other inflation.

Your LA will probably have discussed the impact of the NFF on schools in your area during the last couple of years, so you will probably already know the answer to this question.

If you don't, the provisional allocations file will provide some clues; a new version is released each year. Here are some suggestions on how to interpret your figures within it, using the 2021/22 file mentioned earlier as an example.

You are gaining if:

- Your percentage change per pupil in the last line of the provisional allocations table is greater than the level of the NFF funding floor (which is 2% in the 2021/22 file).
- You have seen some gains in per-pupil funding over the last three years (ignoring changes in pupil numbers). Note that if early gains were capped, the abolition of capping in the NFF in

2020/21 may have caused a sudden big jump, but this doesn't continue once you're at the NFF level of funding; you'll only receive inflationary uplifts.

You are losing if:

- Your percentage change per pupil in the provisional allocations file is equal to the NFF funding floor (2% in the 2021/22 file).
- You have seen a declining per-pupil funding level in the early years of the NFF; the funding floor was set at a maximum reduction of 1.5% when it was first introduced.

Question 4: Do you qualify for Minimum Per Pupil Funding Level protection?

This will only apply to schools with low per-pupil funding in cash terms, usually those with extremely low levels of additional needs. If you're not in this position, you can move on to question 5.

If you do qualify for this protection, note that the minimum levels have increased in the last couple of years, but you'll need to check the new policy paper each summer to find out if they are going to change in the following year. From 2021/22, they have been adjusted to include the transfer of pay and pensions grants paid in 2020/21. The addition is £180 per primary pupil and £265 per secondary pupil.

Happily, this protection is identical under both the Soft and Hard NFF, because all LAs are required to replicate it in the local formula.

All you need to do is check that your cash amount per pupil in each year is no lower than the relevant MPPL, once you've applied your estimated percentage increase. If it is lower, you can use the MPPL cash amount. But be sure to use the correct calculation, as outlined in chapter 7.

Question 5: Do you qualify for the Minimum Funding Guarantee protection?

Your most recent funding statement will tell you if you have qualified for the LA's MFG protection under the Soft NFF. When the Hard NFF is introduced, this will become the national funding floor, with no variation allowed.

Key points

- As long as you observe the important caveats, you can use the provisional NFF allocations file to estimate the percentage change if your school is on the NFF.
- Until the Hard NFF is in place, your LA can take different decisions on the local formula, within parameters set by the DfE.
- Be vigilant for consultations and Schools Forum items during the budget process under the Soft NFF.
- It's important to set an accurate baseline for your per-pupil funding, using the data for the current year's budget share allocation.
- Ask yourself the questions set out in this chapter to identify the best assumptions for your best, middle and worst-case per-pupil funding options from those set out in chapter 9.

9

PER-PUPIL FUNDING PROJECTIONS

Per-pupil funding options worksheet

Your next step is to produce the best, middle and worst-case options for your per-pupil funding over the next three years. This chapter provides summary guidance on how to build this part of the model; the PDF provides detailed examples if you need them.

The baseline calculation you created in the previous activity is the foundation of all three options, so you don't need to repeat it; you can simply refer to it when you build the tables for your three options.

Activity 6: Creating the three per-pupil funding options

- In the per-pupil funding options worksheet, create a heading for your best-case table. Repeat the description and baseline year column headings from the baseline section then add three columns for years 1, 2 and 3.
- Create four rows as shown in the example below.

- Create formulae to record the starting point for each year (the previous year's £ per pupil), the percentage change and resultant multiplier, and the calculation of the updated £ per pupil.
- Make sure the top row figures for Year 1 references the baseline year, while Years 2 and 3 reference the previous year's bottom row.
- Copy the table twice to create your middle and worst-case options and ensure the links to the baseline table are correct. Your baseline figure is the same in all three tables.

Figure 10: Example per-pupil funding option (best-case)

Best Case Scenario: £ per pupil				
	Baseline	Year 1	Year 2	Year 3
	2020/21	2021/22	2022/23	2023/24
	£	£	£	£
Baseline funding amount per pupil	4,080.14	4,080.14	4,161.74	4,244.98
Estimated % change in per pupil funding (enter as %)		2.00%	2.00%	2.00%
% Multiplier for funding		102.00%	102.00%	102.00%
Estimated value per pupil		4,161.74	4,244.98	4,329.88

Consult the PDF if you wish to see the detailed formulae.

For the next stage of your model, our guidance on the percentages to enter in this worksheet is in two separate sections according to whether you are gaining or losing from the NFF (question 3 in chapter 8). Please consult your notes and go to the relevant section.

Options if you are gaining

If you are gaining from the NFF, this section provides some ideas on using the information you've gleaned so far to decide the percentage change to apply to each year under the best, middle and worst-case scenarios. If you aren't gaining, skip to the next section.

These suggestions are only intended to guide your thinking; you still have to use your own knowledge and judgement to decide on the best percentages to use. We can't be held responsible for the results!

We have created two tables, one for the Soft NFF and another for the Hard NFF. In our sample model, we used the Soft NFF for Year 1 and the Hard NFF for Year 2 and 3. If the Hard NFF is delayed, you can extend the principles in the Soft NFF table and anticipate your LA's decisions.

The first table provides some suggestions for the Soft NFF (Year 1 in our example), referencing the 2021/22 percentages as guidance:

Figure 11: Suggested options if gaining - Soft NFF

Year 1 per-pupil funding options if gaining from the NFF			
Soft NFF			
	Best	Middle	Worst
If LA formula is not at NFF:	LA guidance on local % change if available, OR school increase per pupil from provisional allocations file	A realistic increase in between best and worst	Lower end of MFG range, OR mid to high end of MFG range if LA is confident of replicating the NFF protection rate.
IF LA has adopted NFF:	School increase per pupil from most recent provisional allocation file		
	Relevant % in 2021/22 example:		
	Per allocations file for your school		+0.5% low +1%-2% mid to high
	Consider LA intentions and/or past trends if information not available. Check cash amount per pupil meets Minimum Per Pupil Funding Levels.		
	If Hard NFF is delayed:		
	Extend the above into Year 2 with estimated percentages		

Our rationale is that during the period of the Soft NFF, you are dependent on the LA's decisions, and there is no guarantee that you will see the gains promised in the national formula, even if they are trying hard to replicate the NFF. As we've seen, the LA grant includes a cash freeze in some elements, which the LA has to manage across the Schools Block.

Worst-case: for the above reasons, we believe it's still advisable to reflect the lowest possible percentage in your worst-case scenario. You could use the middle or upper point in the MFG range if the LA intends to replicate the national funding floor percentage, which they could still do even if they're not using NFF factor values. Use your judgement to decide what assumptions you are comfortable with. If in doubt, use the lowest point, remembering this is meant to be the worst possible option.

Best-case: If your LA is implementing the NFF in 2021/22, you can be fairly confident in using the provisional allocations file for your best-case option. This is the most optimistic estimate, after all. But if the local formula isn't replicating the NFF, you may wish to be more cautious.

Middle-case: this is best placed somewhere in between the other two, as a more realistic option. The LA's budget strategy work could reveal pressures at a late stage, or your pupil characteristics data and local decisions about formula values might mean you don't get the best-case uplift.

Let's now consider some potential assumptions for a gains situation under the Hard NFF, which we've used for years 2 and 3 in our model:

Figure 12: Suggested options if gaining - Hard NFF

Year 2 and 3 per-pupil funding options if gaining from the NFF		
Hard NFF		
Best	Middle	Worst
If not at NFF in Year 1, school increase per provisional allocations file for that year. OR: If at NFF, estimated % uplift applied to key NFF factors	A realistic percentage in between best and worst	Estimated NFF funding floor percentage
Relevant % in 2021/22 example (but will need to estimate for Y2 & 3):		
School increase per provisional allocations OR +3%		+2%
Adjust and roll forward as early announcements are made annually. Check cash amount per pupil meets Minimum Per Pupil Funding Levels.		

Worst-case: again, we'd suggest a cautious choice, at the minimum protection. With no chance of a lower local MFG under the Hard NFF, you can use the NFF funding floor percentage (the terminology may change).

You might wonder why we'd advise you to use the same worst-case option as a school which is losing from the NFF. Our reasoning for this is that the DfE could change the values for different NFF factors in later years to reflect different priorities, such as deprivation, small rural schools, low prior attainment and EAL. Depending on how significant these characteristics are in your data, and in which direction the values go, you could see a shift in your funding levels per pupil. On the other hand, you might gain from any changes, giving you a better result in your best-case scenario. We trust you can see the value of having three scenarios now!

When you are doing your initial forecasting for years 2 and 3, you will need to estimate the funding floor percentage. It only moved slightly between 2020/21 (1.84%) and 2021/22 (2%), and if we had to speculate, it seems unlikely that it will increase much, if at all, in 2022/23.

There are two main reasons for believing this: the overall DSG cash increase in 2022/23 is slightly lower than in the first two years, and more money could be moved to the High Needs Block once the SEND review is completed. You might think these two issues suggest a reduction is possible, but on the other side of the equation, the DfE has completed the movement of underfunded schools on to the NFF in LA grant allocations, so the extra money allocated in 2022/23 won't be needed for that.

Best case: you need to know if your LA put you on the NFF in Year 1 when it was still the Soft NFF. If they didn't, you could see a higher increase in the first year of the Hard NFF to get you onto it, which is why we say you should check the school-level change in the provisional allocations file for Year 1 (2021/22 in our model).

The important point to note is that once you've reached the NFF, either through your LA implementing it or when the Hard NFF is introduced, any big increases you've experienced won't continue. This is because you'll be reliant upon the inflationary increase applied to the national formula; this was 3% in 2021/22 for the key factors. You'll need to estimate this for years 2 and 3.

It's easy to be afflicted by decision paralysis when faced with so many choices. But we recommend that you go with your initial instincts and just forge ahead with a range of percentages instead of procrastinating over this step. You can review the results once you've combined them with your pupil number forecasts and make some changes if you're not happy.

As long as you state your assumptions, reasoned guesswork is perfectly acceptable for forecasting purposes; remember what we said at the beginning about managing expectations.

Options if you are losing

If your funding is reducing in real terms as a result of the NFF, we will show you how to interpret the available information to decide on the percentage changes for your best, middle and worst-case scenarios. These are only intended as a guide; you still need to use your own knowledge and judgement, and we can't be held responsible for the results!

We have created two tables, for the Soft and Hard versions of the NFF. In our model, we used the Soft NFF for Year 1 and the Hard NFF for years 2 and 3. If there is a further delay, you will need to extend the principles in the Soft NFF table and anticipate your LA's decisions.

Here are some suggestions for the Soft NFF (year 1 in our example), referencing the 2021/22 percentages:

Figure 13: Suggested options if losing - Soft NFF

Year 1 per-pupil funding options if losing from the NFF			
Soft NFF			
	Best	Middle	Worst
If LA formula is not at NFF:	LA guidance on local MFG % OR national funding floor level	A realistic percentage in between best and worst	Lower end of MFG range
IF LA has adopted NFF:	National funding floor level (upper end of MFG range)		
Relevant % in 2021/22 example:			
	+2%		+0.5%
Depending on LA intentions and/or past trends.			
If Hard NFF is delayed:			
Extend the above into Year 2 with estimated percentages			

Worst-case: our rationale here is that you are dependent on the LA's decisions under the Soft NFF, and they could decide to use the freedom to choose a Minimum Funding Guarantee which is lower than the funding floor. It's therefore advisable to reflect the lowest level of protection in your worst-case scenario.

Best-case: if the local formula isn't at NFF levels, ask your LA about the MFG percentage. It's generally reasonable to use the top end of the range, which is equivalent to the NFF funding floor.

The middle-case is best placed somewhere in between the other two, as a more realistic option, as your pupil characteristics data and local decisions about formula values might mean you don't get the best-case uplift.

Let's now consider the possibilities under the Hard NFF (years 2 and 3 in our example):

Figure 14: Suggested options if losing - Hard NFF

Year 2 and 3 per-pupil funding options if losing from the NFF		
Hard NFF		
Best	Middle	Worst
Estimated NFF funding floor percentage	Estimated NFF funding floor percentage	Estimated NFF funding floor percentage
Relevant % in 2021/22 example (but will need to estimate for Y2 & 3):		
+2%	+2%	+2%
Adjust and roll forward as early announcements are made annually. Check cash amount per pupil meets Minimum Per Pupil Funding Levels.		

In all options, the main difference here is that there will be no MFG, so your protection will be at the NFF funding floor level. All three options will therefore be the same if your pure NFF calculation is causing a loss.

When you are doing your initial forecasting for years 2 and 3, you will need to estimate the funding floor percentage. It only moved slightly between 2020/21 (1.84%) and 2021/22 (2%), and if we had to speculate, it seems unlikely that it will increase much, if at all, in 2022/23.

There are two main reasons for believing this: the overall DSG cash increase is slightly lower than in the first two years of the settlement, and more money could be moved to the High Needs Block once the SEND review is completed. You might think this would reduce it, but on the other side of the equation, the DfE has completed the movement of underfunded schools on to the NFF in LA grant allocations, so the extra money allocated in 2022/23 won't be needed for that.

One feature to watch out for is that if your MFG protection has previously been very low, you are nearing the pure formula and will reach it at some point. When this happens, your best-case option could reflect the inflationary increase applied to the national formula; this will be slightly above the national funding floor percentage. You'll need to estimate this for your Year 2 and 3 forecasts.

We recommend that you trust your instincts and try some percentages; don't procrastinate over this step. You can review the results once you've combined them with your pupil number forecasts and make some changes if you're not happy.

As long as you state your assumptions, reasoned guesswork is perfectly acceptable for forecasting purposes; remember what we said at the beginning about managing expectations.

Agreeing the assumptions

Please make sure that you record the reasons for the assumptions you are using to underpin the model. You may be asked to explain them when seeking agreement as you progress through your forecasting exercise.

Key considerations are similar to those we made in the chapter on pupil number projections. The per-pupil part is very technical, and your SLT colleagues and governors may not have much previous knowledge of it, so you will need to try and find a simple way of explaining it that will give them confidence in your grasp of the information.

It is therefore worth devoting time to seek agreement to the assumptions you've made in this part of the model. It will be particularly challenging to unpick it at a later stage if there's a change in key players and/or anyone queries the decisions. Carry your stakeholders with you, and you'll find it easier to get their approval for any later updates as more information becomes available.

If you find yourself having a crisis of confidence in this area of the model, you could test out your thinking with your LA or ESFA contact to check whether they feel your assumptions are reasonable. They should be pleased you are being assiduous in preparing a robust three-year forecast, and I hope they'll be happy to help.

Completing per-pupil funding tables

Well done for working through what is probably the most challenging stage of the model. But it's a crucial one, and when we move to the next stage of combining the options with pupil numbers, you'll see what a difference your assumptions on per-pupil funding can make to your funding forecasts.

This activity involves applying your estimated percentage changes in per-pupil funding in each of the three options.

Activity 7: Completing your per-pupil funding tables

- Return to your forecasting file and insert the percentages for years 1, 2 and 3 in the best, middle and worst-case per-pupil funding tables which you created in Activity 6.
- Test the formulae to make sure the per-pupil funding levels for each year reflect the percentage changes in all the tables.

See the PDF for a completed version.

Adding back excluded items

Earlier, you excluded some items from the calculation of the per-pupil funding baseline in order to achieve an amount per pupil that was mainly driven by pupil data. These are commonly referred to as MFG exclusions, because the calculation follows the Minimum Funding Guarantee method-ology which is based on pupil-led items.

You now need to estimate these MFG exclusions over the period of your forecasts under the best, middle and worst-case options, so that they can be added into your scenarios later on.

It is very important to identify any items that are one-off in nature, and make sure you don't add them into your model, for example:

- If two schools amalgamate, an additional lump sum is paid in the first year to avoid the successor school being immediately disadvantaged by losing one of the two lump sums. The LA may ask the DfE for permission to extend it to a second year, though the amount will usually reduce. If you have received such an amount, make sure you don't continue to count it beyond the allocated time.

- If a school received a split site allowance in the baseline year then is brought on to a single site, the split site allowance will be withdrawn and should not be added back in later years.
- Any changes in funding for exceptional circumstances need to be checked in the same way.

It can be tricky to estimate the changes in excluded items, because some are based on the LA's historic planned spending, and we don't know what will happen to them under the Hard NFF. They may not be significant in the overall scheme of things, so it's best to use your three scenarios to apply a range of changes that you feel you can justify.

You can apply a standard set of percentages across the options. If you want to estimate each one, here are some suggestions.

• Lump sum and sparsity factors

While the Soft NFF is in place, the lump sum and sparsity values should be part of your LA's plans. Whether there are any changes to the local values will depend on how they compare to the NFF values. Some LAs have had to reduce them in either sector or both, in order to replicate the NFF. These values probably won't increase significantly during the Soft NFF period beyond an inflationary uplift, because the high number of schools would make the cost prohibitive. However, they could be reviewed under the Hard NFF. As with all forecasting, as long as you provide reasons for the assumptions you are making, a reasonable estimate is all that can be expected.

• Non-Domestic Rates

If you are an academy, you should not have excluded rates from your baseline calculation, as they weren't included in the first line of your GAG statement in the first place. Add them into your total funding estimate now, using your separate rates allocation from ESFA as a guide.

For all schools, funding bodies are expected to adjust the rates allocation to match actual expenditure. We therefore advise you to use the same figure for both your funding and expenditure. There could be a time lag in the rates adjustment, but over three years this should even out.

Rates could change if your school is expanding to meet the demand for places, if you are altering your buildings, or if rateable values are being reviewed. It can take some time for new rates liabilities to be confirmed, so you may need to contact your LA for advice on the potential changes. Again, make sure the funding and expenditure estimates are aligned.

If you are in the process of becoming an academy or a trust/faith school, your rates will reduce due to charitable rate relief, so remember to adjust your funding and expenditure estimates to match the new cost.

• Private Finance Initiative costs

If you are part of a PFI contract, you should have some guidance from your funding body on inflationary uplifts to the affordability gap costs and any contractual service charges made to your school. The national uplift might not match the local agreements.

• Exceptional circumstances funding

By its very nature, this category is individual to your situation, so you will need to take advice from your funding body on the assumptions you can make. Unless you know it will cease or reduce in the three-year period, it's probably best to estimate a standstill figure for your worst case, and two different inflation percentages for middle and best-case options.

Activity 8: Forecasting excluded items

- Create a table at the bottom of your per-pupil funding

worksheet and list your excluded items. Set out columns for the baseline year and years 1, 2 and 3.

- Decide how many options you wish to create for these items and construct the relevant number of tables to create your forecasts. You will be able to decide how to spread these figures across your final scenarios at a later stage in the process.

Figure 15: Example of excluded items forecast

Excluded items				
	2020/21	2021/22	2022/23	2023/24
Estimated excluded items: future year % change		3%	3%	3%
Rates	12,460	12,834	13,219	13,615
Lump sum and sparsity factors	114,400	117,800	121,334	124,974
Additional lump sum for amalgamating schools (one-off)	0	0	0	0
Any other items, e.g. exceptional circumstances	0	0	0	0
Total excluded items to add back	126,860	130,634	134,553	138,589

See the PDF for the formulae.

***

Key points

- Set up your per-pupil options worksheet, building on your baseline to create three options across years 1, 2 and 3.
- Follow our guidance according to whether you are gaining or losing out from the NFF (question 3 in chapter 8).
- Select the annual percentage change according to whether each year is assumed to be under the Soft or Hard NFF. Be cautious!
- Remember to gain agreement for your assumptions.
- Create forecasts for the items you excluded from the baseline; whether you vary these across three options depends on how significant they are and the nature of the items.

10

COMBINING YOUR OPTIONS

The power of combinations

So far, we have considered the two main elements of your funding separately: the amount per pupil and the number of pupils. You can see the individual impact of changes in your rolls and per-pupil funding for the three different options across the three-year period.

But it's when you start to put together the two elements that you start to see how powerful the interaction is between them. Let's take just one example, so you can start to see the impact of changing rolls on funding.

Figure 16: Impact of roll changes on pupil-led funding

	Best	Worst	Difference	Change at static £ per pupil £4,080.14
Baseline	321	321	0	
Year 1	326	305	-21	(£85,683)
Year 2	330	291	-39	(£159,125)
Year 3	337	282	-55	(£224,408)

Figure 15 uses our fictitious primary school's baseline per pupil of £4,080.14 for 2020/21 before applying any percentage changes. See the changes on a static per-pupil value; you can imagine how rapidly this will change if the £ per pupil decreases from the best to worst-case scenarios.

As you bring together the funding and rolls options, check that the results show a reasonable set of variations. You won't want to spend valuable time debating minor differences between them.

As you will see in a moment, there are nine possible combinations, from which you will choose three to develop into full scenarios. While you are going through this process, think about your level of confidence in your pupil number and £ per pupil options. This will help you select your final three scenarios to develop into budget plans.

Combining the options

Your next activity involves calculating all the combinations of your best, middle and worst-case roll projections and per pupil funding to identify the full range of funding possibilities. You will be mapping them against each other to produce nine possible combinations, as shown in the following table. We're using £ per pupil as shorthand for per-pupil funding in these activities.

Figure 17: Combinations matrix

		Rolls		
		Best	Middle	Worst
£	Best	1	2	3
per	Middle	4	5	6
pupil	Worst	7	8	9

We grouped the three sections according to the £ per pupil values:

- First section: best £ per pupil applied to all three roll options (scenarios 1 to 3)
- Second section: middle £ per pupil applied to three roll options (scenarios 4 to 6)
- Third section: worst £ per pupil applied to three roll options (scenarios 7 to 9).

Activity 9: Setting up the combinations worksheet

- Add a blank worksheet to the file and name it Combinations.
- Create fields as shown in the blank example below for scenarios 1 to 3 to show the pupil-led funding value under each (which you will calculate later), the excluded items and a total budget share forecast line.
- Create a formula to sum the pupil-led funding and MFG exclusions lines under each option.
- Copy the table twice to create the other six scenarios. We grouped the three sections according to the £ per pupil values, firstly matching best £ per pupil against all three roll options (scenarios 1 to 3), then repeating this for middle £ per pupil (4 to 6) and worst £ per pupil (7 to 9).

Figure 18: Example of Combinations worksheet (Scenarios 1-3)

	Baseline 2020/21	Year 1 2021/22	Year 2 2022/23	Year 3 2023/24
Best case £ per pupil funding				
1. Best case rolls				
Pupil-led funding total				
Plus MFG exclusions				
Total budget share	£ -	£ -	£ -	£ -
2. Middle case rolls				
Pupil-led funding total				
Plus MFG exclusions				
Total budget share	£ -	£ -	£ -	£ -
3. Worst case rolls				
Pupil-led funding total				
Plus MFG exclusions				
Total budget share	£ -	£ -	£ -	£ -

We found it helpful to colour the rows for £ per pupil and rolls to make it easier when entering the links. See the pdf for more details.

93

Populating £ per pupil elements

The next task is to populate the best, middle and worst-case £ per pupil lines in your Combinations worksheet, i.e. the first row in each section. You simply need to create links to bring across the correct figures from the per-pupil funding options worksheet.

Once you are confident that your formulae are all accurate, you can lock the cells and protect the sheet (but don't lose the password!).

Activity 10: Populating £ per pupil projections

- In the top line, Best case £ per pupil funding, create formulae to pick up the relevant links for the best £ per pupil figures for each year from the per-pupil funding options sheet. You will be using this line to create scenarios 1 to 3, multiplying it by the three roll projections.
- Repeat the link creation for the first line in each of the other two sections: Middle case £ per pupil funding (scenarios 4 to 6) and Worst case £ per pupil funding (scenarios 7 to 9).
- Be sure to check that the correct figures appear.

Consult the PDF if you would like to follow our example model.

* * *

Populating roll projections elements

The next stage is to populate the roll projections on the numbered rows in all three sections of the Combinations sheet. The best, middle and worst-case rolls are common across all three sections, so you can copy the first set of formulae into the other two sections. This will be easier if you know how to fix the references using the absolute key (F4) to avoid errors. Please double check, to avoid strange results!

Activity 11: Populating roll elements

- In the first row of scenario 1, create formulae to pick up the relevant links from the rolls worksheet for the best roll option for each year.
- Repeat the link creation for the middle and worst-case rolls in scenarios 2 and 3.
- Follow the above two steps for the relevant roll options in the second and third sections (scenarios 4 to 6 and 7 to 9).
- Be sure to check that the correct figures appear.

Consult the PDF for further details.

* * *

Pupil-led funding forecast

Your pupil-led funding forecast is produced within the Combinations worksheet by multiplying together the £ per pupil and roll projection for each option across all nine scenarios over three years. Here's where you start to see the differences between your best, middle and worst-case assumptions.

Activity 12: Calculating pupil-led funding totals

- For each set of combinations, populate the row labelled 'Pupil-led funding total'. Start with scenario 1: multiply the Best £ per pupil at the top by the best-case rolls.
- Repeat for scenarios 2 and 3 using middle and worst-case rolls.

- Work similarly on the middle £ per pupil section (scenarios 4-6) and the worst £ per pupil section (scenarios 7 to 9).
- Check that everything is working correctly.

Consult the PDF for more details.

* * *

Once you have created your formulae, whenever you change any part of your options sheets, everything should update in the Combinations sheet.

You're now well on the way to completing your pre-16 forecasts. The next step is to add in the items that you excluded from your baseline.

Allocating previously excluded items

Now it's time to turn your pupil-led funding forecast into a budget share projection. One decision you need to take is how to spread your excluded items across the nine scenarios in the Combinations worksheet. You are free to choose whatever makes sense. If the items relevant to you are closely associated with pupil numbers, you could have three versions and allocate them in line with best, middle and worst-case roll options.

If you believe there isn't much scope for significant changes to these items, you could use the same figure for all options, as we did in our example model. You might decide only to reflect inflation.

Once you have populated the lines for excluded items, consider whether they look reasonable, given how significant the sums are in the overall context.

Activity 13: Populating excluded items

- In the MFG Exclusions rows of your Combinations worksheet, enter a formula to bring across the excluded items totals from your £ per pupil worksheet. You'll need to decide where to allocate them in the nine scenarios, depending on how far you varied them.

- Double check that the totals for pupil-led funding and excluded items in each scenario are working correctly, and that they look reasonable as budget share forecasts.

Consult the PDF for more details.

Now you have a substantial part of your funding organised into nine potential scenarios, it's a good time to narrow it down to three final scenarios before adding other sources of funding. The next chapter will provide guidance on issues to consider when deciding which three to choose.

Key points

- Combining your options for rolls with per-pupil funding options starts to open up the different possibilities for your future funding.
- This stage will produce nine potential scenarios, from which you will choose three to develop more fully.
- You can set up the Combinations worksheet to draw figures from the roll and per-pupil funding projections sheets, so that any changes made to the original sheets will update automatically.
- Multiply each £ per pupil option by each rolls option to form the nine scenarios as in the example model.
- Add in the previously excluded items to produce nine scenarios for your total budget share.
- The next step will be to choose three from the nine to transfer into your budget planning software.

11

CHOOSING YOUR THREE SCENARIOS

Why three scenarios?

It is nonsensical to even think of producing nine budget plans, so you will need to narrow them down before going any further. We advise you to reduce them down to three before adding other funding streams.

Why three scenarios? Well, three is a sensible number because it allows you to consider the best and worst extremes, balanced by a more realistic and likely scenario somewhere in between.

Another important consideration is that choosing three minimises the amount of work. Any more than this would be unwieldy; let's face it, time is precious and you have to deal with many other important demands.

In practice, you are likely to focus on the middle-case scenario for your medium-term financial plan. But the uncertain landscape in school funding means that there are no guarantees that this scenario will happen. Government decisions are often taken late, and having backup plans at the ready will save you a lot of time and anxiety.

We therefore urge you to keep the best and worst-case scenarios up to date, in case you need to deploy them. In chapter 3 we discussed the benefits of scenario planning, including managing uncertainty and easier decision-making. The whole point of the exercise is to have some high-level alternatives which you can turn to if things don't pan out as you expected.

Try to achieve reasonable gaps between the three scenarios; there is no point in doing a lot of work on alternative spending plans if there's not much difference in the funding they're based on.

We recommend that you spend some time with your leadership team exploring which three combinations you wish to develop further. It's an important decision, as your future strategic financial planning will hinge on these figures. But don't forget it is meant to be a broad-brush exercise. If you have created the right expectations, your fellow leaders and governors won't be anticipating total accuracy.

Part of the value of this approach lies in the discussions you will have about which of the scenarios to choose as your final three. The exercise may expose the real level of uncertainty about the two elements involved. Different members of the team might have different views, and it may take some time to reach a consensus. This will be time well spent, as it will create a common understanding which will underpin future discussions about how to respond to the different levels of funding.

Don't forget to record the discussion; it will provide evidence to support your Financial Sustainability Plan. At a later point, you might collectively change your minds about which three scenarios you are going to develop further as full budget plans. There could be a variety of reasons for this; perhaps you've had second thoughts about your assumptions in the initial exercise, or new information might come to light.

Having the notes to hand can help you decide whether to explore some of the other scenarios instead, especially if circumstances have changed. It will be quick and easy to update your model because of the way we've designed it.

The purpose of this stage is to demonstrate the range of possibilities and make a set of rational choices. In this chapter, we will provide some suggestions on how to choose your final three scenarios.

How to choose your final three scenarios

Here's a reminder of the matrix of nine scenarios from which you will be choosing three to develop further:

Figure 19: Combinations matrix

		Rolls		
		Best	Middle	Worst
£ per pupil	Best	1	2	3
	Middle	4	5	6
	Worst	7	8	9

At one end of the scale, the most simplistic approach can be to match up the two elements like for like across the matrix and choose scenarios 1, 5 and 9. No one would blame you for feeling clueless about both your rolls and per-pupil funding levels!

This is likely to provide a good spread of values from best to worst-case, which is desirable. But a little more thought will give you the best possible chance of three robust alternatives.

One important consideration is that you might not want to give equal weighting to both elements. You don't have to match best with best and so on. Consider how confident you feel about each of the two main elements of your projections. For example, you might want to match up a middle-case rolls option with a worst-case £ per pupil option.

Look back at the information on which you based your roll options. Are your admission numbers relatively stable, with limited in-year movements of pupils across the school? In that case, you're likely to favour scenarios in either the best or middle columns of the matrix.

On the other hand, applications might be volatile and/or pupil mobility could be high. You will then be more likely to choose scenarios based on the worst or middle case columns.

Your choices will then depend on your level of confidence in the £ per pupil options. This is admittedly much trickier if you're not already on the NFF and/or your LA doesn't have a clear strategy for how it will run the formula prior to the Hard NFF being introduced. Again, review the information you considered when choosing your three options.

There's one other thing we'd like to clarify: your final scenarios are relative to each other, so don't worry about how the individual elements are named in the matrix. Just because you need a best-case final scenario, it doesn't mean it has to include a best-case rolls or £ per pupil element. The main thing is to achieve reasonable differentials between them.

Don't over-think it; you can always come back to it and change your mind. In a moment, we'll suggest a lookup table which allows you to simply enter the scenario number and see all the figures change.

Whichever scenarios you choose as your final three, make sure that you place them in order of total funding value from highest to lowest when arranging them in the final scenarios sheet in the next activity. Depending on how significant the percentage changes are for the two elements, the order of the final amounts might not necessarily correspond with the scenario numbers.

Constructing a summary table

We suggest you add a summary table to the model, as a reference point when creating your Final Scenarios tables. This will allow you to test out different scenarios for the budget share part of your forecasts quickly and easily.

Don't worry about the details of how it will work; all will become clear when we get to the stage of creating the Final Scenarios worksheet.

We've found this invaluable as a shortcut when trying to decide which budget share scenarios to choose as the final three, because it avoids constant switching between the Combinations and Final Scenarios work-sheets. You could extend it for your other funding sources if you wish, but they may not be significant enough to warrant it.

The best place to build your summary table is at the bottom of the Combinations worksheet, since that is where all of the information resides that you'll be drawing on.

Activity 14: Building a summary table

- At the end of your Combinations worksheet, create a summary table with one row for each of the nine scenarios, and three sets of columns: per pupil funding, rolls and budget share (the total of pupil-led funding and MFG exclusions). Within each set, show the three years of forecasts.

- Number the columns (you'll see why when you get to the Final Scenarios stage). Your table should look similar to this:

Figure 20: Summary table in Combinations worksheet

1	2	3	4	5	6	7	8	9	10
	Per pupil funding			Roll			Budget share		
	Y1	Y2	Y3	Y1	Y2	Y3	Y1	Y2	Y3
S1									
S2									
S3									
S4									
S5									
S6									
S7									
S8									
S9									

- Create a simple cell reference formula to populate the table with the figures from the combinations table within the same worksheet. Check that the correct figures appear and test it out to make sure that if you change anything in the roll projections or per-pupil funding sheets, these figures automatically update.
- Make sure that you take the budget share before de-delegation figure directly from the combinations table total rows for each scenario. Do not multiply the per-pupil funding and rolls fields within the summary table, otherwise you will omit the excluded items.

Consult the PDF for more details.

* * *

You've come a long way, and the model is building up nicely. But we want it to be as complete as possible, so there is a little more work to do on some of your other funding sources before you can set up the final three scenarios. The next stage is to consider what your other funding streams might look like over the next three years.

Our next chapter will consider the various Pupil Premium grants. If these are not particularly significant for your school, you can produce your own estimates manually. But if it is a large element of your funding, you can use the roll projections you have already prepared as the basis for estimating future Pupil Premium eligibility.

Key points

- Choose your final three scenarios from the nine, based on your level of confidence in the pupil numbers and £ per pupil elements.
- A summary table will make it easier to create a lookup table at the next stage to allow you to test out different scenarios before deciding on three.
- Discuss the results with your SLT colleagues and governors to ensure you have their support. A common understanding will underpin future discussions on how to respond to different levels of funding.
- Remember to record the reasons for your decisions, to make it easier to produce your Financial Sustainability Plan.

12

PUPIL PREMIUM

Pupil Premium categories

The different categories of Pupil Premium have not been affected by the introduction of the NFF, though there are no guarantees for the future.

The individual elements are therefore the same as before: Free School Meals (FSM), Looked After Children (including those adopted from care and care leavers) and Service Children. They all apply only to pupils aged in year groups from Reception to Y11.

There is also an Early Years Pupil Premium for three and four-year olds in early years settings. Unlike the other Pupil Premium grants, this is paid as part of the Early Years Block within the Dedicated Schools Grant.

After a prolonged period of static values, Pupil Premium rates were increased in April 2020. The latest rates can be found at https://www.gov.uk/government/publications/pupil-premium/pupil-premium. They are being maintained in 2021/22.

This page also includes a link to advice from the Education Endowment Foundation on a tiered approach to spending Pupil Premium.

The Pupil Premium Grant (PPG) is paid to the LA for onward payment in full directly to schools and academies (with one exception which we explain below). It is separate from budget share and is not to be included in the calculation of any protection such as the Minimum Funding Guarantee.

We don't know if the current arrangements will continue when the Hard NFF is introduced, or whether the DfE will make the payments directly to schools and academies from that point. Nothing has been said about merging it with budget shares, but such a move would generally be perceived as weakening accountability.

Relevant pupil numbers

Knowing which pupils can be counted is important for your forecasting of Pupil Premium. More details on eligibility and how pupils are counted for each of the categories can be found at the relevant year's page on the conditions of grant.

You can find details for 2020/21 at this link: https://www.gov.uk/government/publications/pupil-premium-allocations-and-conditions-of-grant-2020-to-2021/pupil-premium-conditions-of-grant-2020-to-2021.

FSM Premium (main PPG)

Up to 2020/21, the FSM Premium was calculated for eligible pupils (those flagged as being in receipt of FSM at any census point in the last six years) on the school roll in the January census prior to the start of the financial year. However, for 2021/22, this has changed to the October census. In cases of opening or closure, a pro-rata grant is paid.

Looked-After Premium (also known as Pupil Premium Plus)

This is based on the Looked-After data return (SSDA903) submitted by the LA in March of each year. If a pupil qualifies for this grant, they do not qualify for the FSM Premium as well.

There are two parts to the Looked-After Premium. The first is for children currently looked-after, and is managed by the Virtual School Head in the LA that looks after the child. It must be used to meet the child's educational needs as described in their personal education plan.

The importance of this is that the LA is permitted to retain ('top slice') some of it to provide support directly to individual looked-after children, such as a tutoring service, so the school educating the child might not receive all of the grant.

The second is for children previously looked-after (those subject to an adoption, special guardianship or child arrangements order). This comes directly to the school and cannot be top sliced by the LA.

Every Virtual School is required to publish a clear policy on their use of this grant. You should be able to find it on your LA's education website, or there may be a report to the School's Forum on their decisions about any top-slice of the element for currently looked-after children.

Service Children Premium

The six-year period of eligibility also applies to service children and is based on those on roll in the January census who are recorded as an Ever 6 Service Child or are in receipt of certain armed forces or war pensions.

Early Years Premium

Three and four-year-olds are eligible for the Early Years Premium if they receive the 15 hours entitlement and their families receive qualifying benefits or if they are a looked-after child or a care leaver.

If a child qualifies for EYPP under several criteria, they only attract the funding once. Four-year-olds in reception classes already receiving the school-age pupil premium are not eligible for EYPP funding.

LAs must distribute the Early Years Premium to all early years settings in their area with eligible children at the national hourly rate up to a maximum of 570 hours per year (15 hours per week for 38 weeks). It is paid on the universal 15 hours only, not on the additional 15 hours accessed by working parents.

Assumptions for Pupil Premium Grant

The use of the Ever 6 criterion for the FSM Pupil Premium ensures there is less volatility in the grant allocations. This makes it somewhat easier for you to produce forecasts if you have a relatively stable pupil population, because you can focus predominantly on starters and leavers.

If you have high mobility, you will need to consider whether/how far this changes your eligibility rates.

Your model already contains a starting point for your FSM Premium forecasts, because you have already established your roll projections and a turnover allowance if appropriate. You therefore only need to consider the eligibility rates for different year groups.

Here are a few ideas for you to consider:

- Over the years, shifts in the economy have affected the number of families qualifying for individual benefits that in turn allow eligibility for FSM. This in turn has affected the calculation of Pupil Premium eligibility.
- There is currently some protection for those on Universal Credit, which may last for a long time.
- Locally, you may be aware of changes in the jobs market, e.g. large businesses closing or relocating to or from your area. This may inform your predictions of eligibility for new pupils.
- In many areas, the introduction of Universal Infant Free School Meals has significantly weakened the incentive for eligible parents to apply until the start of Key Stage 2. As year 6 pupils leave, if fewer Reception and KS1 pupils apply for FSM, this may start to affect the overall rate of Pupil Premium eligibility.
- Many schools therefore have to work hard to persuade parents to register. It can be even more challenging for secondary schools, although at least they benefit from several years of eligibility when their students were in primary school.
- Schools with pupils who have recently entered the country may find it even more difficult to establish eligibility. There can be significant delays in benefits being confirmed, and it's difficult to know how Brexit will affect this.

If you are lucky, you may have an LA that is proactive in financial inclusion and provides support to help schools maximise FSM registration, for example through campaigns in the local media.

Many LAs offer an eligibility checking service which uses data sharing permissions to cross-match information with the national benefits system. We find that most schools recognise the time-saving benefits of buying into such a service; it's a common area of de-delegation of funding decided by LA school representatives on Schools Forums and is frequently taken as a buyback service by academies.

For service children and Looked After Children, you will probably want to enter your own estimate of the data for each year directly, as for most schools except those near army bases and in areas of severe deprivation, the pattern can be fairly random. You could use a single estimate for your best, middle and worst-case options for these elements, since the numbers are likely to be small. Do whatever feels appropriate.

Always consider whether the effort you are putting into an area of your forecasts is worth it. Where it will only make a marginal difference to the scenarios, you are better off focusing on other aspects.

So if your Pupil Premium is relatively low, feel free to create estimates outside of the model and enter them directly. Otherwise, continue to the next section, where we guide you through creating a worksheet to calculate your forecasts.

Constructing the Pupil Premium model

For the main FSM Premium, which is sometimes referred to as the Disadvantage Premium, you can save yourself some work by copying the roll projections sheet to use as a starting point. You can then apply eligibility percentages to them as explained in Activity 15, varying them for the three scenarios across the three-year period. Alternatively, you can input eligible pupil numbers directly.

Activity 15: FSM Premium forecasts

- Create a copy of your roll projections worksheet and rename it Pupil Premium.

- Insert a section to show the funding rates at the top of the sheet; you can show separate values for the three years if you wish to make any assumptions about changes in the rates across your scenarios.
- Extend each scenario by adding rows below the roll data and entering the estimated eligibility percentage in years 1, 2 and 3 by year group or key stage. If you expect the percentages to be stable across the period, use a single row.
- In the rows for eligible pupil numbers, multiply the rolls by the eligibility percentage for the three-year period.
- Create cells with formulae to multiply the total eligible pupils for each year by the relevant funding rate. This will allow you to see the impact of your pupil number changes and assumed eligibility rates on your projected FSM Premium grant.
- The table below shows our example worksheet for the FSM Premium best-case scenario with other categories added.

Figure 21: Pupil Premium scenarios

												R-Y6 total	Estimated funding primary	Estimated funding LAC	Estimated funding service	Total Estimated funding
Pupil Premium scenarios																
			Primary	Secondary	LAC	Service										
Funding rates 2020/21 (can estimate future years/scenarios if you wish)			£1,345	£ 955	£2,345	£ 310										
1. Roll projections - best case scenario																
			R	Y1	Y2	Y3	Y4	Y5	Y6							
Baseline	2020/21	Oct-19	44	42	38	44	50	52	51	321					
Year 1	2021/22	Oct-20	48	48	44	39	44	50	52	326					
Year 2	2022/23	Oct-21	48	53	51	45	39	44	50	330					
Year 3	2023/24	Oct-22	48	53	55	52	45	39	44	337					
Turnover allowance				10%	5%	3%	0%	0%	0%						
Ever 6 eligibility			19%	20%	22%	20%	25%	24%	25%						
Baseline	Eligible pupils 2020/21		8	8	8	9	13	12	13	71	£95,495	£11,725	£620	£107,840
Year 1	Eligible pupils 2021/22		9	10	10	8	11	12	13	73	£98,185	£11,725	£620	£110,530
Year 2	Eligible pupils 2022/23		9	11	11	9	10	11	13	74	£99,530	£9,380	£0	£108,910
Year 3	Eligible pupils 2023/24		9	11	12	10	11	9	11	73	£98,185	£7,035	£0	£105,220

- Repeat the above process to create two more tables for your middle and worst-case FSM Premium scenarios.
- Review the results to check that you are happy with the estimated grants shown. Are the differences between the scenarios reasonable, given your circumstances?

The PDF shows all our workings.

We suggest that for the remaining categories of Pupil Premium, you create a table at the foot of the worksheet and enter your forecasts manually for the three scenarios over the three-year period. The numbers will be relatively low and are easily calculated. You can then total all elements ready to be transferred to a Final Scenarios worksheet once you've examined other sources of funding.

Key points

- Pupil Premium categories have not changed since the introduction of the NFF, but you should watch for any future announcements.
- Use the link to the DfE's Pupil Premium webpages to check the eligibility conditions in order to forecast the number of eligible pupils and decide on variations for the three scenarios across the three-year period.
- For the FSM Premium, you can use a copy of the roll projections worksheet and add eligibility fields to calculate your best, middle and worst-case options. Use an approach that is proportionate to the level of your Pupil Premium grants.
- Consider any local economic changes which might affect your assumptions on eligibility. Check if your LA provides any guidance or helps to maximise FSM applications.
- The remaining categories are likely to be less significant and you can enter your forecasts for the three scenarios directly into the worksheet.

13

OTHER FUNDING SOURCES

Forecasting other grants

So far, we have focused on your core funding — budget share or the main component of academy General Annual Grant — and Pupil Premium. You will also need to include forecasts of other funding across the three-year period, to cover all funding streams on which your expenditure is based.

In this chapter, we are focusing on grant funding, **not** self-generated income which you will offset against expenditure in your budget plan.

We will help you identify those grants which are relevant, but bear in mind that they may change in future years. It is challenging to predict what might happen, because grant regimes may change as the government decides to fund different priorities. They can issue new grants, move existing ones into core funding (e.g. pay and pensions grants), or cease funding streams at short notice (e.g. Y7 Catch Up funding).

Be watchful for any announcements. Our School Financial Success blog and newsletter will help you to identify any significant changes and your funding body should also draw attention to them.

Here's one important reminder: **you must not incorporate pay and pensions grants for teachers into this section** of your model. You have already added them into the per-pupil funding baseline, reflecting the grants being transferred into the Dedicated Schools Grant from 2021/22. The protections have also been adjusted to ensure that the existing allocations are guaranteed to remain.

While reading this chapter, think about how you want to show your other sources of funding in the model, ready for when you build the final worksheet. You will need to make your own decisions on this, as the range of grants that different schools are eligible for makes it difficult and possibly unhelpful to be prescriptive.

Remember only to include grant funding. Do not include self-generated income such as lettings, fund-raising from non-government sources, donations or sales income. These items form part of your net expenditure which you will be comparing against the funding, so if you include them in funding you will duplicate them.

Significance of other grants

It may not be necessary to take the same comprehensive approach that we used for your core funding when attempting projections of other grant funding. How significant is the level of funding for each of your sources outside of budget share or the core component of GAG?There is little point in doing detailed work if the monetary value is relatively low.

A reasonable stab at best, middle and worst-case patterns over the three years may be sufficient for these other sources.

Not all of the sections in this chapter will be applicable to your situation, so you will be able to skip some of them, for example if you don't have a nursery or sixth form.

Nursery funding

For schools with nursery provision, funding can be volatile. The market for early years places is subject to many influences, and sometimes there is over-provision. Allocations of free entitlement funding are provisional, based on estimated annual hours, until the relevant termly census data is available. Adjustments are made during the year to reflect the actual children taking up entitlements. There are also multiple streams of funding in addition to this.

It can therefore be challenging to forecast nursery funding even within the current year, let alone for a three-year forecast. But essentially the same elements drive your funding as for the main school budget share: the amount per pupil and the number of pupils.

The main difference is that in the case of nursery funding, multiple headcounts are used rather than a single annual census. When updating provider budgets during the year, local authorities must either use the total number of hours across the year or a count based on at least three different weeks during the year. Many authorities use termly counts.

You can use the same principles to develop your nursery funding forecasts as for the main school budget, but you probably don't need to go as far as preparing nine options. Nursery funding is likely to be a relatively small proportion of your overall funding unless you are a first school with early years provision, so you could choose just three options: best, middle and worst-case combinations of hourly rates and take up. But you will want to pay attention to any fluctuations in take-up across the three terms.

Feel free to work out a model that is tailored to your own circumstances, perhaps using some elements of the main model. This section includes information for you to consider when making your assumptions.

Because it's helpful to understand the context of the funding, we'll start with a brief run-down of the national formula for early years. This is used to calculate the grant paid to local authorities for onward distribution to all nursery settings. These include not only nursery classes in schools, but also maintained nursery schools, childminders, private/voluntary/independent (PVI) settings, and playgroups.

Early Years National Funding Formula (NFF)

The Early Years NFF relates to the universal fifteen-hour entitlement for three- and four-year-olds. The totals generated by the NFF factors for each local authority are divided by the number of hours taken up, creating an overall hourly rate. This is individual to each LA. A local early years formula has to be in place and LAs must pass 95% of the funding for this age group to providers.

Funding for the extra 15 hours in the 30-hour entitlement for working

JULIE CORDINER & NIKOLA FLINT

parents is paid to LAs at the same rate as the universal entitlement, and LAs have to mirror this consistency in their local formula.

Transitional arrangements are in place to move LA funding levels towards the Early Years NFF, just as for the main Schools NFF. Over time, each LA's funding should move towards the national average. However, it will take a considerable time for some to get anywhere near it, especially in London and other areas with historically high hourly rates.

If you are a primary school and have a Maintained Nursery School (MNS) in your local area, it's worth being aware of the issues surrounding the NFF for these settings, because if they are unable to continue, you could be asked to take their children. The problem lies in the creation of a universal rate for all types of early years settings. MNSs generally have higher unit costs, on account of the requirement to have a headteacher and a designated deputy in what is usually a relatively small setting. The fact that MNSs don't have economies of scale is not recognised in the Early Years NFF, unlike the Schools NFF where small rural schools have a sparsity factor.

To address these problems, Supplementary Funding has been given to MNSs over the last few years (and continues in 2021/22), pending a full review of the situation. If this protection is ever removed without making substantive changes to the Early Years NFF, many nursery schools could close. If you have one nearby which is at risk, you will need to assess the potential impact if you are asked to fill the gap in provision, especially if the universal hourly rate in your local area doesn't fully cover your costs.

Roll projections for nursery children

Estimating the take-up of nursery entitlements is one of the more challenging aspects of forecasting your funding. The use of termly headcounts (the method chosen by most LAs) with payments adjusted in arrears can cause volatility, especially in areas where there is strong competition between providers.

As with roll projections for 5-16 year olds, you need to base your best, middle and worst-case options on a set of reasonable assumptions. The best you can do is to look back at trends then consider any known population changes likely to occur in your area alongside your local knowledge about parental preferences.

Having good links with playgroups and childminders can help, but don't forget the influence of grandparents, who may be the ones bringing children to nursery, as they do for pupils further up the school. Some nurseries attract pupils on the basis of travel-to-work patterns, which can be even trickier to forecast in the current economic climate.

Your LA should prepare sufficiency assessments for early years places, which may reveal unmet demand or over-provision in your area. You will be aware of any younger siblings of pupils already in your school.

The part-time nature of school nurseries and the limitations on being able to offer fully flexible places can affect take-up. In some areas, there are good links between private, voluntary and independent settings (PVIs) and school nurseries. This helps to meet parental needs by facilitating full-day provision. This may give you more confidence about the likelihood of places being filled. However, in other areas there is high competition between providers, causing instability in the 'market' for pupils. It all needs to be considered when developing nursery roll projections.

Be aware of the basis of your LA's definition of part-time or full-time equivalents, depending on how they present the eligible pupil numbers for nursery provision. The government provides funding for 15 hours for 38 weeks in the universal entitlement. Check if your LA follows this when combining your £ per pupil funding with roll projections to produce your forecasts. Some LAs may fund 39 weeks, taking PD days into account.

You will need to produce three different levels of pupil numbers for your best, middle and worst-case options, and record the reasons for your assumptions.

Nursery per-pupil funding

As with the Schools NFF, nursery funding only partly depends on government decisions. A local formula operates, which must treat all types of provision in the same way. However, there are no proposals for direct funding of early years by the DfE, so you don't have the complication of a Soft and Hard NFF in this area.

This means that it's important to be well-informed about your local early years formula. Keep an eye on your Schools Forum website for agendas, reports and minutes, or try to attend meetings as an observer, particularly in the second half of the autumn term and early spring term. The LA may hold sector consultation meetings.

You should be made aware of any local proposals to alter nursery funding rates; LAs are obliged to carry out consultations for significant changes. The 2020 Spending Review (SR) has provided extra funding to increase the hourly rate in 2021/22. Beyond this, we have to wait for the next SR. We advise caution in estimating hourly rates over the three years.

As 95% of funding for 3 and 4-year-olds has to be passed to providers, the level of the hourly rate should be fairly stable once your LA reaches the pure formula.

The government has specified a list of factors which is more limited than those for the Schools Block, so Early Years formulae tend to be simpler. Some LAs use only the two mandatory factors: a basic hourly rate and deprivation, while others also incorporate some or all of the discretionary factors: rurality/sparsity, flexibility, English as an Additional Language and quality (workforce qualifications or system leadership).

In developing your best, middle and worst-case scenarios for nursery funding per pupil, you will need to consider how your local factors might affect your funding, and whether your data is changing for each of them.

Funding for disadvantaged 2-year-olds

A similar formulaic approach is used to fund disadvantaged 2-year-olds. This sits outside the NFF, but it is a simpler formula, and LAs are encouraged to use a flat rate when funding these pupils. This aspect should therefore be fairly straightforward, with most of your variation coming from changes in eligible pupils or LA decisions to alter the single rate.

Other funding for early years

a) Early Years Premium

As already mentioned, the Early Years Premium grant is accounted for within the Early Years DSG rather than the separate Pupil Premium Grant. There is usually a comprehensive list of eligibility criteria in the operational guidance for LAs. You can find an example for 2020/21 in section 8.1 of the guidance document at https://www.gov.uk/government/publications/early-years-funding-2020-2021. This document also includes information on how Universal Credit affects eligibility for the EY Premium.

b) SEN Inclusion Fund

Your LA is required to operate a SEN Inclusion Fund (SENIF) for 3 and 4-year-olds with SEND, paid as top-up grants from within the Early Years allocation. This is intended to provide for lower-level SEND, since EHCPs are funded from the High Needs Block. There is no requirement to provide an Inclusion Fund for disadvantaged 2-year-olds, but some LAs do allocate funding for them.

The DfE has not specified any values for the SENIF; each LA will decide how to make allocations from the overall Early Years Block, but they could also make a contribution from the High Needs Budget. You should know if you are receiving this type of funding.

c) Disability Access Fund

The Early Years Block also includes a Disability Access Fund (DAF). LAs are required to pass on the allocation in full to settings with children who fulfil the eligibility criteria: being in receipt of Disability Living Allowance and accessing the 15-hour entitlement. They do not have to take up the full 570 hours of the free entitlement. The value has remained at £615 per eligible child up to 2020/21, but please check for any updates beyond this. Early Years funding policy announcements tend to happen later than the main school funding notifications. The DAF allocation per eligible pupil is a lump sum and should not be pro-rated for part-time attendance.

Once it reaches the setting, this grant does not have to be spent on the eligible children; it can be used to improve facilities so that the setting can take more children with disabilities in the future. If a child moves to a different setting during the year, the funding doesn't move with them; the next setting can only claim it from the start of the following financial year. If a child is splitting their free entitlement between two or more settings during the week, the grant goes to the one nominated by the parent as the main setting.

Inclusion Fund and Disability Access Fund allocations can be included in either the separate line for SEND funding or the Early Years line within the model. We recommend that you make a note of which approach is taken, for future reference. Please double check that you haven't included them twice!

One last point to remember is that you shouldn't include any income from extended childcare in your funding forecasts. This is classed as self-generated income and it should be deducted from your gross expenditure when calculating the net expenditure in your budget plan.

Sixth form funding

Funding for sixth forms is part of the post-16 funding arrangements which also apply to FE colleges and other settings to fund study programmes for individual students. As for pre-16 allocations, it is based on a national formula. Each year, the government updates this. You can see the information for 2020/21 at https://www.gov.uk/guidance/16-to-19-funding-how-it-works.

There are other comprehensive documents on different aspects of the post-16 funding system at the 16-19 funding guidance page which is at: https://www.gov.uk/guidance/16-to-19-education-funding-guidance. However, your forecasts are intended to be broad brush. Unless you have a very large sixth form and/or this is a significant proportion of your total funding, it's probably not advisable to go into too much detail.

Sixth form student number projections

The number of students on roll is obviously key to your forecasts. Your LA should produce pupil population data, but young people usually have a greater choice of education settings at 16 in a local area, so it carries less weight than for pre-16 admissions.

Are you in an area where there is high competition for students? You will already be familiar with the Y11 to Y12 conversion rate from your own school and the intake from other schools in your area. Look back at previous trends and try to assess how they might change in the light of any changes in the local population of this age group.

As well as forecasting basic student numbers, you should consider the number of students re-sitting English and Maths exams, who attract extra funding.

If you are creating new sixth form provision, you should be aware of the phased calculation for funded numbers when considering the pattern of funding across your three-year period:

- Year 1 - one third of capacity
- Year 2 - double actual recruitment in year 1
- Year 3 - lagged numbers.

The situation may be different for academies funded on estimated numbers with new sixth forms, where funding is agreed with the ESFA.

Per-student funding

After a long period of static funding levels per student, at last the government announced an increase in 2020/21. You can see a table with the rates for different categories at this link: https://www.gov.uk/guidance/16-to-19-funding-information-for-2020-to-2021.

The 2020 Spending Review (SR) promised to maintain core funding rates in real terms for 2021/22, i.e. allow for inflation. We have to wait for the 2021 SR for decisions beyond this, so we advise caution in all three options for sixth form funding over the three-year period.

Other elements to bear in mind are student retention, the number studying subjects with higher programme weightings, and levels of disad-vantage. These will all influence your average funding per student. You can control some aspects of these funding elements, but not all of them. Retention can be improved by better advice when students are choosing their subjects, and by monitoring progress in Y12 to pick up any signs that they are struggling or disengaging. But there are many external reasons that you can't control.

High Needs funding for post-16 students should be included in the SEN funding section of your forecasting model; our next section goes into more detail about this area. Apart from place-led funding provided by the ESFA, the remainder relies on allocations from the local authority.

Funding for SEND

If you've read any of our blogs or listened to any of Julie's conference presentations on funding for SEND, you'll know that we have serious concerns about the impact of the High Needs NFF. The formula is not responsive to changes in need, and many LAs have substantial cumulative High Needs deficits. Schools are feeling the pressure of providing support for pupils with SEND in the context of inadequate funding in all of the blocks within the Dedicated Schools Grant, especially (but not exclusively) where they are receiving the minimum increase through NFF protection.

The government has limited the ability of LAs to make transfers from mainstream school budgets to address the SEND funding shortfall; no more than 0.5% can be taken from the Schools Block each year and it requires the approval of the Schools Forum. Any request for a higher transfer has to be approved by the Secretary of State, even if the Forum approves.

Decisions on transfers are difficult, because mainstream schools are not exactly awash with cash. However, when LAs are trying to prevent or reduce a High Needs deficit, moving money from the Schools Block shares the problem more equitably. If LAs have to manage within a ring-fenced High Needs Budget, the savings they will inevitably need to make are likely to penalise schools with specialist provision and those who are inclusive.

This situation caused the government to require all LAs to carry out a review of their High Needs budgets and publish a report on the outcomes, which should be on your LA's Local Offer website. Reviews should all have been completed by now, although the scale of the deficits suggests a likelihood of continuous attention.

If you read your local review report, you should be able to see the LA's proposals for change. These could include intentions to vary the mix of provision and/or set different thresholds for decisions on where pupils' needs can be met throughout the system, with the consequence that mainstream schools are asked to take and keep more pupils with SEND. Reducing high-cost places in the independent sector is likely to be a major focus. Some LAs may also be reviewing the banding systems used to determine top ups.

How can you find out what's happening and anticipate the impact of changes to the local high needs funding system on your school? LAs should have been holding consultation meetings and surveys during their reviews, and the topic will probably have been an agenda item at various network meetings. There should also have been reports to the Schools Forum and to elected members.

The Local Offer website for your area is the best starting point; any reports, consultation materials and presentations should be published there. Otherwise, consult your Schools Forum website and ask your Forum representative about the outcome of any debates on LA proposals.

SEND in mainstream classes

Within your budget share or GAG allocation, an element is notionally labelled as being for low-level SEND: the 'notional SEN budget'. This is **not** an extra allocation; it's simply a part of the overall total allocated, and is a theoretical figure. You have already included this in your model within your budget share.

To calculate the notional SEN budget, LAs decide that a percentage of certain factors within the local funding formula can be deemed to cover low-level SEND, but they can all choose different percentages and indeed different factors.

The most common factors selected are low prior attainment, deprivation indicators, and the Age Weighted Pupil Unit, also known as the basic entitlement (on the basis that every classroom teacher will encounter some degree of SEND), but any factor can be included.

The DfE's High Needs operational guidance indicates that schools are expected to fund additional support for pupils with SEND costing up to

£6,000 per pupil per year from this notional SEN budget. The £6k figure is over and above the ordinary cost of the child being a member of a mainstream class, which the DfE assumes costs £4k per pupil. The two together are equivalent to the £10k per place paid to special schools. If the cost of support for an individual can't be managed within your budget share allocation, you can ask the LA for an additional amount, known as top up funding.

You don't have to spend all of the notional SEN budget on SEND; it isn't ring fenced. But if you are inspected, and outcomes for pupils with SEND are not as they should be, you will be held accountable and questions will be asked. LAs may ask you to explain how you've used it if you apply for top up funding, because the parlous state of High Needs budgets means they can't afford to duplicate funding.

The majority of top ups in mainstream classes will be for pupils with an Education, Health and Care Plan (EHCP), and you should be well aware of these. But some LAs also pay top ups for pupils without plans as part of an early support or inclusion strategy. Bear in mind that this could change following an LA's High Needs review.

There is a situation where mainstream schools can claim additional top ups, which many schools aren't aware of. It's for highly inclusive schools who can prove that they have a higher than average number of pupils with SEND, and that it costs more than the notional SEN budget to support them. It may not be easy to achieve this extra funding allocation, given the pressures LAs are under, but that shouldn't stop you from trying.

Taking all this into account, you should be able to estimate how much you are likely to receive for pupils with SEND in mainstream classes over the next three years. But please take care to remove top up estimates at the right time for pupils who are due to leave the school.

SEN units and resource bases

If you have an SEN unit or resource base (LAs use a variety of names for these), you will receive budget share for the pupils in the unit, plus £6,000 per occupied place and a top up value for costs beyond this. If there are empty places, they are paid at £10k rather than £6k, because there are no pupils to attract budget share/GAG.

If you have an SEN unit or resource base, you should be aware of any proposals to change its designation or size. This could be an outcome from your LA's High Needs Review implementation plan.

LAs can negotiate lower top ups for pupils registered in SEN units and resource bases in two situations: firstly, where they want to place a child above capacity, on the basis that fixed costs have already been covered, and secondly where children are placed into empty places, on the basis that the school has effectively received £10k for a place that hasn't been filled for a substantial part of the year. Some LAs have been driven to introduce this approach if it hasn't previously been the practice, because funding is not keeping pace with needs.

Any such decisions could affect your funding forecasts, so make sure you have all the facts and can reflect any likely impact in your estimated SEN funding within the model.

Basis of top up calculations

For both specialist provision and mainstream classes, the top up calculation is usually based on the actual number of days the child is on roll, because the funding has to follow the child if they move during the year. But you will need to check your own LA's practice.

You are advised to examine trends in top up payments from the last couple of years, and to watch out for relevant children who are approaching a transition point. These will help you decide the levels of top up funding to build into your final scenarios.

If you have children with an Education, Health & Care Plan (EHCP) placed at your school by an LA outside of your local area, their home LA is the commissioning authority and must pay the top up funding. Some LAs have an arrangement to work together to avoid schools having to deal with multiple councils and can agree to use the provider LA's rate for consistency. If this is not the case, you may find that you receive varying top up rates from different LAs for children with similar needs.

Funding for Early Years SEND

In the Early Years section at the start of this chapter, we mentioned

Inclusion Fund and Disability Access Fund allocations. These may be quite small amounts, but don't forget to add them into the SEN or Early Years funding line, whichever you prefer, in your Final Scenarios worksheet when you reach that stage of the model. Just make sure you only include them once!

Growth funding

Schools and academies that are expanding to meet population growth at the request of the LA, i.e. to meet basic need for school places, may qualify for support from the local Growth Fund.

Growth funding sits within the NFF but is not included in the provisional allocations because the data isn't available until the October census before the start of the financial year. LAs are, however, provided with a tool to estimate it in the autumn term to help them develop their budget strategy. Officers need to do early planning to ensure sufficient places, so you should be informed if you are likely to be eligible for growth funding.

LAs should consult the Schools Forum on the qualifying criteria for growth funding and the method of calculating allocations. There are two choices. The first is to use the Growth Fund for 'bulge classes' and other temporary growth; this will be based on selected formula factors such as the basic entitlement and/or a lump sum.

The second method is to adjust pupil numbers in the local formula for new and growing schools, opened in the last seven years, which are adding year groups. This ensures their funding is on the same footing as existing schools on a permanent basis, because the pupils then attract all pupil-led factors in the formula. If your LA confirms that they will be using this method for your school, you can build in the estimated additional pupils.

Funding to support falling rolls

In recent years, some LAs have had a Falling Rolls Fund to support schools which struggle to deliver the curriculum because of declining pupil numbers. This is not intended to support falling rolls caused by parental preference, and it is only available for good and outstanding schools where there is a temporary dip and the places will be needed in the future. This avoids an LA having to close a school, then incurring high costs to open a new one a couple of years later.

However, the grant previously awarded to LAs for this fund is no longer available. Instead of separating it out, the DfE added the money to the Growth factor, allocating it using the growth criteria. This means that if you previously received funding for falling rolls, your LA will no longer be getting any grant for it from the DfE. Officers can decide to maintain a local fund from the growth allocation. If you are in this position, we advise you to check whether your LA is still making payments and ask them if you will continue to qualify.

Other grants

The categories of funding to be added into the model under the heading of 'Other grants' will vary, depending on your type of school and the multi-year period under consideration.

Grants other than those we have already mentioned are likely to be time limited, so you should check the likely timescales and exclude them if there is a risk that they might cease during the three-year period. It's better to be cautious, especially in your worst-case scenario.

You should have an exit strategy for any temporary grants and be prepared to put it into action in your multi-year budget plan if necessary. Secondary and middle schools will have had to adjust their funding estimates for the Year 7 Catch Up Premium, which was suddenly withdrawn when the government announced the Covid Catch Up Fund.

Tracking the grants to include

Announcements on changes in government grants can be found on the gov.uk website, and you can sign up for ESFA bulletins which usually draw attention to changes in grants or rates of funding. But a less time-intensive way to keep up to date is to sign up for our own free School Financial Success monthly newsletter, as already mentioned.

Your multi-year budget plan will predominantly focus on revenue funding and expenditure, so it should only include revenue grants. But you will want to keep a separate record of capital grants and expenditure in order to identify any cross over, such as the need to make revenue contributions to capital projects in your expenditure plans. It doesn't work the other way; you cannot use capital funding for revenue purposes.

We can't predict all the grants which will be available during the three-year period you are working on, but they could include some of the following:

- Primary PE & Sport Premium
- Universal Infant Free School Meals
- Grants for school improvement
- Multi-academy trusts: pre- and post-opening grants and capacity grants for those taking on additional schools.

Local authorities sometimes have a Schools in Financial Difficulty fund. Although it's not possible to extract the amounts from published financial information, anecdotally this type of fund seems to have fallen out of favour. Schools Forums can be reluctant to agree to it; heads who have taken difficult decisions to manage their budgets may oppose a proposal to take money out of the formula for this purpose.

Adjustments to funding

There are some other items which are not grants, but rather adjustments to your funding after budget share has been determined. They are mostly deductions, such as for de-delegation of specified services (LA schools), exclusions, and the DfE's Risk Protection Arrangement. You can also see a positive adjustment if you admit excluded pupils.

Our first instinct was to incorporate these items into the funding forecasts. However, guidance and the frameworks for Consistent Financial Reporting (CFR) and the Academies Accounts Return (AAR) require them to be shown as expenditure. If you include them in your funding forecasts, you would have to remember to exclude them from your budget plans. This would be potentially confusing and would require an adjustment to your reconciliation when compiling your return.

We would therefore suggest that to keep it simple and avoid double counting these items, you show them as expenditure or income in your budget plans, and ignore the adjustments in your funding forecasts.

When the Hard NFF is introduced, de-delegation of services for LA maintained schools is likely to cease when the Hard NFF is introduced. If LAs and schools still want the services to be centralised, it's likely to switch to an individual school decision, as currently happens for academies, special schools and PRUs. So dealing with it as expenditure is probably appropriate for the longer term as well.

MAT top-slicing of GAG is dealt with at trust level, but if you are an academy in a MAT with autonomy over finance and are carrying out your own forecasts, you may choose whether to reduce your funding forecast by an estimated amount, or deal with it in the expenditure and income part of your budget plan. Just make sure you don't do both!

Key points

- You will need to incorporate all funding sources on which your expenditure is based.
- We have provided guidance to help you develop assumptions for nursery provision, sixth forms, SEND, pupil number growth and other specific grants.
- Do not include self-generated income, which is part of your expenditure plans.
- Do not include teachers' pay and pensions grants, as they are already in your budget share baseline.
- Avoid spending too much time developing detailed forecasts for low value grants.
- Where adjustments to funding are classified as expenditure in guidance for various returns, we suggest you exclude them from your forecasts.

14

PREPARING YOUR FINAL SCENARIOS

Drawing it all together

You've persevered through all the stages of building your scenarios and considering the different funding streams that you need to include. Congratulations! Now you can bring everything together in a set of three complete final scenarios for your total funding.

So far, you have whittled down your nine options for core funding to three scenarios. You've identified best, middle and worst-case values for all other funding, considering the number of eligible pupils or expiry dates for any time-limited grants. The end result should reflect an agreed set of robust assumptions which can be defended should anyone challenge them.

Now it's time to create the final forecasting document which draws everything together into a single sheet, summarising all your hard work.

Constructing the final scenarios

The last stage is to create a Final Scenarios worksheet to display your complete set of funding forecasts.

If you set up this new sheet with a VLOOKUP function referencing the summary table in the Combinations worksheet, you will be able to test out different budget share scenarios. By simply entering a scenario number, all the correct data for your budget share line should appear, as long as your formulae are accurate!

The other sources of funding aren't covered in the lookup table (unless you choose to extend it), so you can enter them in the last stage.

Activity 16: Preparing Final Scenarios

- Set up a Final Scenarios worksheet with three tables for best, middle and worst-case scenarios. Include a field for a scenario number in each table. See Figure 20 for an example.
- Create a VLOOKUP formula (see below) to bring across the per-pupil funding, rolls and budget share values from the summary table in the Combinations worksheet when a scenario number is typed into the Final Scenarios table.
- Repeat the process for the middle and worst-case scenarios, making sure you refer to the individual scenario number cell in each table.
- Test your formula by entering different scenario numbers in the Final Scenarios sheet and checking against the Combinations summary table to ensure that the results are correct.

The downloadable PDF shows the formulae based on our sample model. There are three parts to the VLOOKUP function:

1. Lookup value: the scenario field in the Final Scenarios worksheet, e.g. S1, that you want to tell Excel to find in the Combinations sheet summary table.
2. Table array: the full range of cells in the Combinations sheet summary table that you want Excel to search in, to find the values to populate the relevant Final Scenarios cells.
3. Column index number: the number you've recorded at the top of the column that you want to take the data from. If you

number all the columns in the summary table from left to right, it's easier to find the correct one for each cell. If you have any blank columns in the table array range, you must number them.

Figure 22: Final Scenarios worksheet (scenarios 1 to 3)

		Scenario reference	2021/22	2022/23	2023/24
	Best case	**S1**			
1	Per pupil funding	£4,080.14	£ 4,161.75	£ 4,244.98	£ 4,329.88
2	Roll	321	326	330	337
3	Budget share/GAG (before de-delegation/top slice)	£1,436,586	£1,485,865	£1,536,173	£1,598,398
4	Pupil Premium				
5	Nursery funding				
6	Post 16 funding				
7	SEN funding				
8	Other grants (list in detail)				
		1,436,586	**1,485,865**	**1,536,173**	**1,598,398**
	Change year on year		49,279	50,309	62,225
	Cumulative change		49,279	99,587	161,812

* * *

You are very close to finalising the model now. The next step is to complete the remaining lines of the table to incorporate all other funding streams.

Activity 17: Recording other sources of funding

- If you have created a Pupil Premium model or any worksheets for other funding streams, enter a formula to bring them into the Final Scenarios tables, or if not, insert the values manually.
- Allocate your other funding sources to the best, middle and worst-case scenarios. We advise showing a detailed breakdown.
- Make sure that the totals in the Final Scenarios worksheet pick up the correct rows for your total funding across the three-year period for each of the three scenarios.

* * *

You will probably want to return to this section of your funding forecasts on a regular basis, as further information becomes available on the government's intentions for different funding streams.

Your budget share figures will automatically update as you change your roll projections or the percentages in your per-pupil funding sheets. The lines that require manual alterations will be the other funding sources.

Sense checking

We encourage you to review the results in your Final Scenarios worksheet to make sure that they look sensible. Have you included the correct rows in your totals? Do the scenarios go from a higher figure (best-case) down to a lower figure (worst-case)? If not, consider swapping round some scenario numbers.

Remember the purpose of the exercise, which is to compare three different funding levels. If there isn't much of a difference between them, it won't be worth the effort to develop budget plans for each one. If this is the case, review your assumptions and see if you need to create more of a variation across the different elements.

Do your other sources of funding look reasonable? Have you been over-optimistic? Do your assumptions stand up to challenge? Make sure they are robust; it's advisable to test them out with SLT colleagues before talking to governors and consider their views carefully.

Make careful notes of the assumptions underpinning the choice of your final scenarios. In some cases, particularly the other funding streams, there may be a direct link to your expenditure plans, which will help you in firming up your budget.

For example, if any of your funding is ring-fenced, i.e. can only be spent on a specific purpose, you will need to match up the expenditure on those functions with the grant estimates when constructing your multi-year budget. Our book 'School Budget Mastery' goes into details about different types of funding and how they should be treated. You should carefully check the conditions of all grants to identify where this could be an issue.

Periodic review

You have now reached the stage when you can put the results into your budget planning software to identify whether any issues have arisen in relation to your current spending plans. Your normal approach to budget setting takes over at this point, but it will be far better informed, because you have put some thought into the potential changes that could happen in each of your three scenarios.

It's tempting to complete the process and forget about your forecasts. You'll want to focus on deciding how to respond to any gap that emerges between the funding in each scenario and your spending plans.

But circumstances change, and it is advisable to make a note in your diary to carry out a termly review of the assumptions, updating the model if necessary. From time to time, you should also check whether your final three scenarios are still the right ones.

Obtaining approval

You will have done a lot of thinking about the assumptions that underpin the model; this may have produced some significant debates. The work you've done will help your fellow leaders and governors to understand the potential for external changes to affect your school's financial position in the future. But you will still need to go through a formal approval stage to fulfil governance requirements.

There should be no need to fear this stage, because of the preparatory work you've done. As we discussed in one of our earliest chapters, it will have highlighted the levels of uncertainty you are dealing with, and will hopefully have relieved some of the pressure on you to provide accurate figures. The situation is far from clear cut, and the method you've followed will help to emphasise that fact.

Having led the debate about the assumptions and having risk assessed them to ensure that they stand up to challenge, you will be well equipped to use the scenarios as the basis for your multi-year budget plan.

The level of detail in the model should give assurance to your funding body that you have taken the responsibility of multi-year financial planning seriously. You have focused on the strategic issues while paying attention to detail, using all the intelligence, both hard data and soft information, to good effect. This work can only enhance your standing as a leader within your school, academy or MAT.

You now need to convey the results of your work to staff, governors and other interested parties, according to your governance model. This will include the funding forecasts and any actions needed to bring expenditure in line with the available funding under each of your final scenarios.

Securing agreement to a set of responses for these circumstances will mean you are better prepared for any eventuality. As more information emerges to indicate which of them is likely to be the final version, you will be able to commit to the actions; in fact, you may already have taken some early steps towards them.

One effective way to present your findings and highlight the actions needed is to produce a Financial Sustainability Plan. This will set out the process you have gone through and the conclusions you have reached. You may have your own version of this, but if not, our next chapter will outline an approach and a suggested template for you to get the message across.

Key points

- Create a Final Scenarios worksheet with a VLOOKUP function to draw figures from the Combinations summary table. This allows you to enter a scenario number and see the budget share figures appear automatically.
- Test out different scenarios before settling on your final three.
- Add in the other funding sources and complete a sense check for accuracy.
- Make sure that there is enough difference between your final three scenarios to justify the effort of creating budget plans for them.
- If necessary, revisit your assumptions until you are satisfied that they are robust and produce a reasonable set of alternative funding forecasts.
- Make sure you have agreement from SLT colleagues and governors, and record the rationale for the final decisions.

15

YOUR FINANCIAL SUSTAINABILITY PLAN

Purpose

The purpose of a Financial Sustainability Plan (FSP) is to draw together the elements you have considered in forecasting your school's funding, show how you have produced your multi-year budget projections and explain the conclusions you have reached. It will include an action plan outlining how solutions can be implemented to resolve any anticipated shortfall, or how additional resources can be used wisely to support school improvement.

You are aiming for a succinct, coherent and presentable document which can be used to explain your financial strategy to a variety of interested parties such as governors, senior leaders, your funding body and Ofsted or other relevant inspectorates.

The FSP should be a working document which is rolled forward annually and updated on a regular basis, especially when there is a significant change that affects either your funding or spending plans.

The need to update the funding elements might result from a change in pupil numbers since your initial estimations, a change in the government's policy on school funding or the announcement of the settlement for the forthcoming year. You might have new information relating to expenditure which will significantly affect your multi-year budget plans. You need to make a judgement on whether the changes are material enough to warrant an update during the year.

Whether updated mid-year or not, this working document should be used continuously throughout the year. The purpose of the FSP as far as senior leaders are concerned is to inform strategic decision making. It should be referred to whenever you are taking decisions on staffing, reviewing the curriculum or producing your school development plan for the year ahead.

Linking all your plans is essential to help you achieve value for money. Integrated Curriculum-Led Financial Planning is a useful technique to assess your teaching staff deployment and test affordability. Your FSP helps to bring together all aspects of the school's planning processes, linked to your overall vision.

For governors, the FSP provides an important insight into the school's medium-term planning, giving a solid evidence base and assurance that backs up the decisions you are asking them to take throughout the year. For funding bodies and Ofsted, the FSP gives a reassurance that the school is a going concern and that performance can be sustained into the future.

Benefits of an FSP

A Financial Sustainability Plan gives you an opportunity to present your medium-term financial plans to your staff, governors and funding bodies with a greater degree of confidence about the level of funding you may receive in the future. It sets out clearly the school's financial strategy, explains the assumptions you have made in reaching your conclusions, and allows you to share the evidence on which they are based.

The FSP should be relatively easy to compile, because you have already completed the groundwork on funding forecasts by following the process in this book. The notes you have made throughout will be invaluable in speeding up the process. Your plan provides a structure for collating everything you have done so far into one professional and coherent document.

It can also be quickly and easily updated each time your funding forecasts and/or multi-year budget projections are updated, to give context to the plans as they change.

This book relates to the funding part of your FSP, the missing part of the multi-year financial planning jigsaw. If you need guidance on the income and expenditure part of your budget, our books 'School Budget Mastery' and 'Leading a School Budget Review' provide in-depth information.

Suggested structure

The basics

It is important to make your FSP look professional. Simple things will make a big difference, such as a title page with your school logo, the name of the document (Financial Sustainability Plan), the years it covers and the date of preparation (with version control). If you have a corporate style for your school improvement planning documents, adopting it will signal that the FSP is an integral part of a suite of planning documents that collectively drive the school forward.

Ensure you use clear page numbering, as you may need to jump around the FSP when you are presenting it and you want your audience to be able to keep up with you. Include a contents page with links to each of the sections. It's a simple step, but without this you run the risk of the reader becoming lost and not understanding the structure of the plan.

MATs may need to consider whether to produce separate plans for each academy or show the overall plan in a single report.

The content

While you are free to decide your own structure, the main sections we would expect to see in a Financial Sustainability Plan are:

1. Introduction
2. Approach to multi-year funding projections
3. Best, middle and worst-case scenarios for future funding

4. Comparison of future funding with current expenditure plans
5. Multi-year Budget Plan
6. Action Plan
7. Appendices

The detail

1. Introduction

You may choose to write your own introduction, explaining what an FSP is and its purpose in the context of your school. We have provided a sample introduction in an appendix, which you may use and tailor to meet your own needs. This is generic enough to be used for any school. Importantly, it sets the scene for the reader to gain an understanding of what the FSP is trying to achieve.

2. Approach to multi-year funding projections

The purpose of this section is to explain how you have constructed the forecasts of your funding to facilitate the production of the multi-year budget projections. Here you need to describe the process you have been through in following the activities and be very clear about the assumptions that underpin them.

You should provide a rationale for your choices at each stage of the model, accompanied by clear evidence. Show how you have consulted colleagues and specialists in order to obtain relevant information and how you have applied it to the key elements within the model.

Soon you will see how important it is to include the results of the activities you have undertaken as appendices to your FSP, in order to provide an evidence base for your assumptions and conclusions. This is the section where you will describe what you did and reference those appendices.

You may experience challenge and debate when presenting your FSP;

this should be welcomed as part of the ongoing process. It will allow you to review and refine your funding projections where necessary.

Because this section will be strongly tailored to the context of your own school and the assumptions you have made, we can't provide a generic example of how you might display your workings for the different options and combinations in your appendices.

You can take screenshots of your own model and insert them as images, as we've done for our accompanying PDF document.

3. Best, middle and worst-case scenarios for future funding

Here you will include the summary of final scenarios across the three years to show the outcome of your modelling. You could show the full nine options in an appendix, if you want to emphasise the range of possibilities.

You will provide notes that draw attention to particular issues or features, explaining the reasons for your final choices. This section will move the reader from the general principles and assumptions described in the previous section to specific aspects of the final scenarios you have chosen.

It's advisable to make it clear that these scenarios can be amended as further information becomes available. You could indicate the sort of circumstances that might make this necessary or desirable.

This section can conclude with a clear statement of the best, middle and worst-case funding forecasts.

4. Comparison of future funding with expenditure plans

This section is very important and will be specific to your school's circumstances. It will show what happened when you compared your future funding with the school's current expenditure plans. Crucially, it will highlight any significant gaps between the resources that you expect to receive over the multi-year period and what you currently plan to spend.

Note that you should have updated your current expenditure to allow for estimated future pay awards and any other known variations in cost. You are creating an 'as is' expenditure profile, i.e. the future cost of your existing set-up, before you consider the impact of funding changes in the next section of your plan. This would include any residual impact of Covid-related pressures or savings, depending on your situation.

The conclusions you draw in this section naturally depend on the outcome that you experience, i.e. a shortfall, a match or a surplus. You need to quantify the extent of any savings needed or any surplus funding that might be available under each of the scenarios.

An accompanying commentary will be needed, to explain what each scenario is showing and what this means for your school; this is an essential part of the FSP. It will reassure your audience of the depth of your understanding, aid their own comprehension and add deeper meaning to the plans.

You may also want to include any details of assumptions you have made in your current expenditure plans, as these will eventually influence or limit the solutions in the next section of your plan. A particularly important element will be your estimate of future pay awards for teaching and support staff. Also worthy of consideration will be the impact of the government's decision to transfer grants for the September 2018 and 2019 teaching awards and pensions increases into core funding from 2021/22.

We recommend that you describe here any provision for other known cost pressures. Remember that the School Financial Success monthly newsletter and blog, noted in the 'Keep in Touch' pages of this book, are good sources of information on government policy announcements.

As with the funding forecasts, be prepared for challenges on your expenditure and have your evidence ready for a detailed discussion. Achieving consensus will be vital in order to make the next stages of the process work.

These matters can be presented in any format that you feel appropriate for your school and the way you work. They could be taken directly from financial forecasting software reports or you may choose to produce your own using spreadsheets.

The aim of this section is to set the baseline position, i.e. showing what would happen if your funding forecasts came to fruition and you had not acted but had maintained expenditure at the current planned levels.

This sets the scene for the next section, where you identify strategies to make good any shortfall or allocate any surplus wisely to support your school improvement strategy.

5. Multi-year Budget Plan

This part of the FSP represents your response to the funding changes. In this section, you need to present your suggested solutions for any antici-pated reduction or increase in funding and show the new version of your multi-year budget for each of the three final scenarios. While the best and worst-case scenarios are less likely than the middle-case, you need to agree how you would respond if they did become a reality.

If your school is facing funding challenges, leaders and governors will need to agree what the solutions might look like. Alternatively, if addi-tional funding is a likely scenario for you, how might you deploy this funding? Have you quantified the cost pressures that need to be covered first?

Remember that these projections are only estimates. It is important to be prepared; you may be hopeful that your funding will increase, but until that becomes a reality, you should not spend in anticipation of what is not yet realised.

Similarly, be careful that your potential solutions are not overly pessimistic. At present they are only a possibility. In some cases, you may start implementing them early, but in others you simply need to know what your solutions will be, should you need them.

We advise creating a timeline plan setting out the solutions for each of your three final scenarios. You may need to prove to your funding body that a time-limited recovery plan is feasible if there is any risk of the school falling into deficit.

Whilst staffing is likely to be the main area of consideration for any required savings, there may be other areas of the budget which can become more efficient.

Apart from staffing, are there any areas of budget expenditure that could be easily reduced with little or no impact on the quality of education your school provides? Even if some negative impact is unavoidable, is this preferable to reducing staffing levels? Can income generation be pursued more vigorously?

When asking yourself these questions, remember always to consider the principles of value for money. Pay particular attention to the impact that you expect to see from existing or reduced spending in each area. For detailed advice and guidance, see our book, 'Leading a School Budget Review'. It deals with the cultural issues as well as the practical processes for examining all the areas within your budget.

Your school's response to potential funding changes is probably the most difficult part of the process you have embarked on. We advise using the FSP to involve the rest of your senior leadership team in developing solutions. This is a strategic school improvement planning process, not just a budget exercise, and one member of staff shouldn't be left to handle it alone, even if they have an overall responsibility for finance. The view of all senior leaders is critical to securing the appropriate response to support your school's continuous improvement.

6. Action Plan

Your action plan will be tailored to your school, detailing the next steps you need to take in order to achieve a sustainable budget. This is the culmination of all your work so far, using the information you have prepared and the proposed solutions to identify specific actions which need to be taken by named individuals.

The action plan should clearly show the responsibilities of individuals and teams, as well as some indication of the timelines for all of the key actions required to achieve the necessary changes in your budget.

The actions should be specific, organised within broader headings such as staffing restructures, re-negotiation of contracts and income generation strategies.

Be clear about the expected outcomes from each action and show how, by whom, and at what intervals progress and completion of the action plan will be monitored. Knowing how you will take corrective action if the plan is not on target is important.

Don't forget to identify any resources that will be needed to make the action plan happen. Some solutions may require a small investment in order to secure savings. You must be able to identify the impact in each financial year as a basis for your three-year budget.

7. Appendices

Your appendices should contain the outputs from the activities you have worked on throughout the book. These will build a sound evidence base for the information you are presenting in the main body of the plan and we strongly recommend that you include them.

Here is a checklist of the worksheets you will complete in the process, to guide you in your list of appendices:

- Roll projections worksheet;
- Per-pupil funding worksheet;
- Combinations of per pupil funding and roll projections (budget share forecasts);
- FSM/Disadvantage Premium forecasts (if used);
- Your own worksheets for nursery, post-16 and other Pupil Premium funding, plus any other funding sources as applicable;
- Final scenarios bringing everything together.

For the sections relating to your multi-year budget plan, you will have an existing format for your budget reports. Consider whether this is fit for purpose in the light of what your FSP shows; could it be presented more clearly? Is it meaningful and clear to the reader?

Incorporating other financial information

You may find that your FSP becomes a useful report in which to record other important financial information which feeds into your overall financial strategy. Examples could include results from financial benchmarking, Integrated Curriculum Financial Planning (ICFP) work and the Schools Resource Management (SRM) self-assessment. If you decide to do this, consider the level of detail you would include. Think about who will read the plan and what they need to know. The section on 'Using Your FSP' will help with this.

Updating and refining the plan

Your multi-year budget projections should be updated at least annually, but it may be necessary to amend them mid-year if new information becomes known that would make a material difference and affect your overall financial management strategy.

We recommend that you develop an audit trail of any changes made and the justification for them. At a later date, you or other leaders may need to identify the reasons why a different approach was taken.

When you make an update to your multi-year budget projections, the following parts of the FSP may need to be updated to reflect the change:

1. Introduction: an explanation of why the update is needed.
2. Approach to multi-year funding projections: any changes to the assumptions you have made.
3. Best, middle and worst-case scenarios: replace any that have changed, including the selection of different options for the final three.
4. Comparison of future funding with current expenditure plans: re-calculate the differences if the changes significantly alter your school's overall position, from a surplus to a deficit or vice versa, or if there is a change in the projected level of funding.
5. Multi-year budget plan: review your interpretation of any significant changes to projections to accommodate any movement in your financial position.
6. Action plan: update actions in accordance with any significant changes in the overall picture for your school and check whether the timeline is still realistic.
7. Appendices: update the relevant worksheets in your appendices if any of the changes relate to your funding forecasts or expenditure plans.

Using the FSP for financial leadership

We talked about the concept of financial leadership at the start of this book. Essentially, financial leadership is about all leaders having ownership of and shared responsibility for the school's finances in a strategic sense.

This means having an awareness of the school's financial position, understanding how the school's financial plans link to all other school improvement plans and getting the financial culture in the school right, by role-modelling desired financial behaviours.

The FSP is a key element in achieving strong financial leadership in your school. It helps to make some of the complex issues and challenges your school is faced with more understandable and it provides a real insight into what lies ahead.

Involving senior leaders and governors throughout the process of forecasting your school's budget, particularly when estimating your future pupil numbers, encourages challenge and debate, deepening their awareness and understanding.

For schools whose financial position is challenging, the FSP may trigger a fundamental budget review, the process for which we explain in detail in our book 'Leading a School Budget Review'. It is essential that staff are engaged in the process of a school budget review to secure its long-term success. The FSP provides solid evidence to persuade interested parties that a school budget review is needed and gets buy-in from staff from an early stage.

You will be conscious of the need to report the information you have to the Governing Body. There are a number of reasons for this, but primarily the Governing Body holds school leaders to account for pupil outcomes, overall school improvement and achieving a balanced budget. The FSP is an effective way of presenting the information.

Remember that you will also need the Governing Body's approval to enter into a consultation with staff for a staffing reduction, if this is needed. The earlier the Governing Body are aware that this is a possibility, the more understanding and supportive of this proposal they should be.

The FSP can also be a useful tool in discussions with unions in a restructuring situation, as you will be able to prove that your proposals have emerged from a thorough consideration of the options.

Presenting your plan

Always provide your audience with the FSP prior to the meeting in which you present it. For governors, this should be ideally be seven days before the meeting. They will need time to digest the information, to enable them to make any meaningful challenge and to contribute to the debate during the meeting.

You may be worried that the information could be difficult to understand and even intimidating for some, without the context that you would provide in your face-to-face presentation. Assure colleagues or governors that you will present the information in full at the meeting and will answer any queries or questions they may have to give the appropriate background information.

If you follow our guidance to develop your FSP, it should be clear enough for most people to get to grips with. You may be concerned about the content itself; for example, one of your multi-year budget projection scenarios may indicate a future potential deficit. It is still wise to give your audience time prior to the meeting to understand the document, but when you send it out you may want to point out in your accompanying correspondence that the detail of the figures needs to be understood within the context of the full explanation that you will provide at the meeting.

When presenting the plan to governors, senior leaders or any other audience, it is important to get the balance right between pessimism and optimism. If you are overly pessimistic in your approach, you may influence colleagues to react with a cost cutting strategy which may involve staff redundancies that don't turn out to be necessary.

If you are too optimistic, the opposite may happen, which could cause a different set of problems. If the need for a staffing review is ignored in the hope that the school won't actually end up in that position, the school could find itself facing a deficit position without sufficient time to restructure and make the necessary savings. This could result in more punitive cuts than an earlier and more measured approach.

A health warning is needed when presenting your information, to explain that a broad-brush approach has been used and that the forecasts are subject to a number of variables which could change. The emphasis should be on planning ahead at an early stage, in order to buy school leaders time to think strategically and sensibly about their response.

The FSP can help you to plan ahead in order to prevent a potential deficit position in the future, or it may guide you in considering how you would use additional resources. Either way, you should think carefully before implementing either strategy and ensure that you are confident in the component parts of your forecasting. You can allow for a margin of error and tailor the action plan as you become aware of any changes in your funding forecasts.

Having a plan will make you better prepared for any unexpected events, because you will know the direction of travel to follow and will not have to take decisions from scratch. You can re-read our chapter on scenario planning as a reminder of all the benefits.

Key points

- A Financial Sustainability Plan draws together your findings to show how you have produced your multi-year funding forecasts and budget projections. It will help others have confidence in your financial strategy to deal with any potential shortfall in funding or invest any possible surpluses for better outcomes.
- Your notes from following the process in this book will make compiling the funding section of the FSP easier. We provide a sample structure for your plan.
- Remember to keep the plan under review and update it to reflect any changes in government funding policy or your assumptions about funding or expenditure.
- Present the plan to SLT colleagues and governors with a realistic outlook and encourage them to debate the solutions to address any funding shortfalls.

16

IN CONCLUSION

Forecasting funding is the one thing that many schools have not attempted, due to the lack of firm information, yet it can make a significant difference to the robustness of your budget projections. The DfE recognises that scenario planning is a helpful technique, and recommends it in school resource management guidance. We hope you've found our approach helpful.

Having gone through this process, you will have a much better under-standing of the influences on your future funding. You have given careful thought to the possibilities and the risks they might pose, and you have challenged yourself to make sure your assumptions are robust. As further information becomes available, it will be easy for you to update the model.

You are taking an important and proactive set of steps towards finan-cial sustainability, and this will raise your profile as a responsible, thoughtful and intelligent leader.

We welcome feedback, so please get in touch with any thoughts you have on the process, especially if you can think of any ways of improving the model, or if you have found it particularly valuable in securing agree-ment from senior leaders and governors to take action to prevent a deficit.

We wish you the very best of luck in securing financial sustainability with a more robust set of funding forecasts.

KEEP IN TOUCH

May we ask a favour? If you have enjoyed reading this book, we'd be very grateful if you could spare a moment to leave a review on the site where you purchased it. This increases the book's visibility, helping other school leaders to find it and benefit from the advice.

The best place to keep in touch and find out about plans for other books in the School Financial Success Guides series is at https://schoolfinancialsuccess.com. It's where you'll find Julie's monthly blog and up-to-date details of books and online courses.

On the School Financial Success home page there's a red button to sign up for Julie's free monthly newsletter. It contains all the government announcements in the previous month relating to finance and funding in education and schools, with a brief explanation and links to the original items.

Here are the links for School Financial Success on social media:

- Facebook page: https://www.facebook.com/SchoolFinancialSuccess/. 'Like' the page to make it more visible in your feed.
- Twitter: https://twitter.com/juliecordiner.

APPENDIX 1: SAMPLE INTRODUCTION TO FINANCIAL SUSTAINABILITY PLAN

Uncertainties in future funding for schools, particularly with the introduction of the National Funding Formula (NFF), and the increasing cost pressures schools are facing, mean that early financial planning for the future is critical to a school's financial success.

The purpose of this Financial Sustainability Plan is to:

- ensure and prove continued value for money education;
- provide an indication of the future financial position to leaders and governors
- Indicate the school's position in terms of a 'going concern', which is particularly important to academy audit teams.

This can involve the following, depending on local circumstances in any given period:

- awareness of future funding possibilities;
- a high-level plan to respond to changes in funding;
- the efficient and effective use of available resources;
- prompt action to avoid a deficit budget, or if unavoidable, preparation of a deficit recovery plan.

The Financial Sustainability Plan details a variety of strategic assumptions about future funding, which is the missing piece of the financial planning jigsaw. It culminates in a series of multi-year budget projections for '(ENTER SCHOOL NAME, or names if a MAT)'.

These budget projections are based on scenario planning techniques which produce best, middle and worst-case scenarios for funding forecasts. They are used as the foundation of a series of multi-year budget projections. The Financial Sustainability Plan is designed to inform future financial planning and decision making for school leaders and governors.

The background work that has been carried out by school leaders to inform this plan is thorough and detailed. All activities undertaken can be found in appendices to this report. The main body of the plan focuses on the multi-year budget projections, interpretation of these different funding scenarios, response to funding changes and an action plan for financial leaders.

Optional (if ICFP and SRM self-assessment have been included):

Also included are results and interpretations of the work carried out in relation to Integrated Curriculum-led Financial Planning (ICFP) and the School Resource Management (SRM) self-assessment. This provides statistical evidence of the school's resource management linked to staffing and curriculum provision. Consideration of these, alongside funding forecasts and multi-year budgets, creates a whole body of financial planning evidence on which to base strategy and decision-making.

ABOUT THE AUTHORS

Julie Cordiner
Education Funding Specialist

I'm a qualified accountant and independent consultant specialising in school funding and education finance, with over thirty-five years' experience in local authority education work, including ten years as an Assistant Director. Between 2007 and 2015 I was a member of the DfE's advisory group on school funding. I advise schools and local authorities on school funding and achieving value for money in order to support better outcomes and enable children and young people to maximise their potential, something I'm passionate about. Everyone deserves the best possible education, and we all need to use taxpayers' money wisely, to achieve a fair chance for every single pupil.

Nikola Flint
Chief Financial Officer

With a background in accountancy and nineteen years' experience in the school business management profession, I fulfil a broad, strategic role as Chief Financial Officer in a multi-academy trust, leading on all aspects of school organisation and SMSC. My experience as a Specialist Leader of Education offering school-to-school support has widened my perspective of the challenges faced by schools and the potential solutions to those challenges. I passionately believe that every child has the right to a high-quality education and that we all have a part to play in achieving this ideal.

Printed in Great Britain
by Amazon

79122975R00092